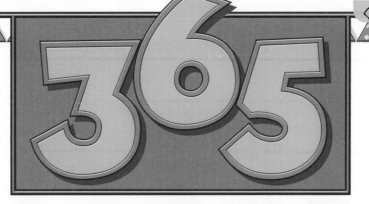

365 AFTER SCHOOL

ACTIVITIES

Contributors:

Marilee Robin Burton

Kelly Milner Halls

Lise Hoffman

Consultant:

Susan A. Miller, Ph.D.

Illustrator:

George Ulrich

Publications International, Ltd.

Louis Weber, CEO
Publications International, Ltd.
7373 North Cicero Ave.
Lincolnwood, Illinois 60712

Manufactured in U.S.A.

8 7 6 5 4 3 2 1

ISBN: 0-7853-4364-4

Marilee Robin Burton holds a master's degree in early childhood education and is a former editor for Scholastic Inc. She has taught in the New York City public school system and has developed materials for various educational publishers, including "On Your Own Books" and "Take Home Books."

Kelly Milner Halls is a freelance writer whose work frequently appears in *Highlights for Children*, *US Kids*, and *FamilyFun Magazine*. She is former coordinator of the Longmont (Colorado) YMCA after school daycare program.

Lise Hoffman is editor in chief of *Child Life* magazine and former editor of *Humpty Dumpty's Magazine* and *Children's Playmate* magazine. She collaborated on *Mathemagic*, a computer book for children, and is a member of the Educational Press Association of America.

Susan A. Miller, Ph.D, is a professor of early childhood education at Kutztown University. She is the former director of preschool and after school daycare programs in Reading, PA. She is author of *Games, Giggles and Giant Steps*; *Learning Through Play: Sand, Water, Wood and Clay*; and has published articles in *Childhood Education*, *Parents*, and *Parent & Child*.

CONTENTS

INTRODUCTION

• • • • • • • • • • • • • • • • • • •

Each project has also been rated with a difficulty level. The number of symbols indicates how difficult the activity is.

Basic skills needed.

Intermediate skills needed.

Advanced skills required.

What Parents Need to Know—

365 After School Activities sounds like a huge number of things to do to interest your child and to keep him or her busy for many hours. But remember that the process is as important as the project! In each activity, children will learn or sharpen skills. They will learn responsibility for their materials and how to clean up after themselves. They will learn creative thinking skills as they combine a new idea with another. They will practice hand and eye coordination—which are necessary school skills as well as life skills. And they will increase their attention span, too!

This book encourages skill building through projects and games. The book is divided into 10 chapters: Posh Projects, Celebrate Life, Fabulously Fit, Helping Hands, Great Games, Dynamic Digits, It's So Yummy, Media Mania, Scientific Sleuthing, and Imagine That! Each project or activity includes a list of what you'll need and easy-to-follow directions. Take time to go over the instructions with your child.

These rating are simply a guide, however. You know your child best. The activities should be fun and enough of a challenge to be exciting for the child. On the other hand, you do not want to frustrate your child with activities that are beyond him or her.

Adult supervision is not needed for many projects in this book. Again, you know your child; some 6-year-olds may need help with projects that 10-year-olds can do by themselves. Many projects just need a watchful eye; some projects need no adult help. It is best if you and your child review the project together and then make a decision about your role.

This should be an enjoyable, creative, energizing experience for your child. Encourage your child to create their own versions of projects and activities, using their own ideas. And don't forget to admire their wonderful results!

What Kids Need to Know—

Although we know you'll want to get started right away, please read these few basic steps before beginning.

1. For any project or activity you decide to do, gather all your materials, remembering to ask permission first! If you need to purchase materials, take along your book or make a shopping list so you know exactly what you need.

2. Prepare your work area ahead of time. Cleanup will be easier if you prepare first!

3. Be sure that an adult is nearby to offer help if you need it. An adult is needed if you will be using a glue gun, a craft knife, the oven, or anything else that may be dangerous!

4. Be careful not to put any materials near your mouth. Watch out for small items, such as beads, around little kids and pets. And keep careful watch of balloons and any broken balloon pieces. These are choking hazards—throw away any pieces immediately! Small children should not play with balloons unless an adult is present.

5. Use the glue gun set on the low-temperature setting. Do not touch the nozzle or the freshly applied glue; it may still be hot. Use the glue gun with adult permission only!

6. Wear an apron when painting with acrylic paints; after the paint dries, it is permanent. If you do get it on your clothes, wash them with soap and warm water immediately.

7. Cover any surface you work on with newspapers or an old, plastic tablecloth if it could be damaged. Ask an adult if you're not sure whether to cover the kitchen table—but remember, it is better to be safe than sorry!

8. Clean up afterward, and put away all materials and tools. Leaving a mess one time may mean that Mom says "No" the next time you ask to make something!

9. Have fun and be creative!

POSH PROJECTS

Relax. You've been bending your brain all day. Switch gears and try making something cool and creative. These Posh Projects just might be the break you need. You'll find terrific gift ideas for family, friends, and furry pets; everyday useful things, such as zipper pulls, book covers, and birdhouses; wearables and jewelry; and decorative items. And there's more where those came from. Be careful, though. Some of these projects are so cool your friends may want you to keep making more and more of them!

A GREEN "VALENTINE"

This is a heart-shaped valentine you can give all year-round. And plants last longer than candy!

What You'll Need: Table covering, small or medium-size pot, potting soil, spoon or small trowel, ivy plant, ruler, a roll of florist wire, scissors, red ribbon

Cover the table you will be working on. Pot the ivy according to the plant directions. Measure and cut three 40-inch-long pieces of florist wire. Match up the ends and twist the 3 pieces together into 1 strand. Bend the twisted strand of florist wire into a heart shape, with the loose ends forming the V at the bottom of the heart. At the bottom of the V, twist the ends together, leaving about a 5-inch "stem" to stick into the potting soil. Stick the heart into the pot near the base of the plant. Tie a red bow at the top of the heart. Loosely wrap strands of the ivy around the heart.

"RECORD" ACHIEVEMENT

When you want to recognize someone for a major achievement, surprise them with this!

What You'll Need: Newspaper, inexpensive 8×10-inch picture frame and cardboard liner, discarded music CD, acrylic gold paint, paintbrush, small game pieces or metal charms, clear gel glue, white paper, pencil, low-plush velvet fabric remnant, gold glitter marker, rubber cement

Spread out the newspaper, and lay the CD and the picture frame on it (use the glass of the frame for some other project). Set the cardboard liner from the picture frame aside. Paint 1 side of the CD and the frame gold. When the frame is dry, use clear gel glue to attach the metal trinkets to the outside of the frame. While the trinkets dry, trace around the cardboard liner on white paper. Cut this out, and use it as a pattern to cut out the velvet.

Practice writing on velvet scraps with the gold glitter marker. Plan what to write. Be brief! You will write the name of the person receiving the award first, then the kind of award. Brush the backside of the velvet and the front of the cardboard liner with rubber cement. Then put them together and let dry. Next, use the rubber cement to glue the CD to the top center of the velvet (be sure there is enough room around the edges to put this piece into the frame). Write the award information on the velvet with the marker. Let the words dry, and put it into the frame. Surprise your super-achieving friend!

TEES, PLEASE

You don't have to be a great artist to make a terrific T-shirt.

What You'll Need: Cotton T-shirt in any color; pictures cut out from printed fabric (the bigger, the better) of cars, aircraft, horses, stuffed animals, flowers, etc.; scissors; dual-sided fusible interfacing; iron; fabric paint in tubes; wide piece of cardboard

Wash and dry the T-shirt first; don't use fabric softener. (Fabric softener keeps the interfacing and paint from bonding completely.) Cut out the pictures and other shapes from the fabric. Plan your original design. Then cut out interfacing to match the fabric pieces. Iron the interfacing onto the fabric pieces following package instructions. (Have an adult help you use the iron.) Then iron the fabric pieces onto the T-shirt. (To make the shirt even more durable, an adult could use a sewing machine to make small stitches around each picture.) Slip the cardboard form into the T-shirt to make the fabric taut before painting. Using fabric paint in a tube, outline all edges of the pictures. This helps anchor them to the T-shirt. Let the paint dry, and then outline the edges again. Let dry for 24 hours. Avoid using fabric softener in the wash later, because it could loosen the fabric pictures.

MIXED-UP MENAGERIE

Make your own private zoo of mystery animals—and name them if you can!

What You'll Need: Chenille stems in lots of colors and thicknesses, pencil, index cards, markers

With the chenille stems, make animals you are familiar with. Then make—and name—the mystery animals. Do a little mixing and matching, and create an animal with a giraffe's neck, a tiger's body, and a monkey's tail—or whatever you can come up with! Round shapes can be made by twisting the chenille stems around pencils and compressing the spirals. When the menagerie is complete, make name cards for each animal with index cards and markers. Invite visitors to admire your experimental zoo!

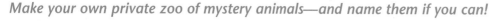

ZIPPER CHIC

5

These are easy, believe it or knot! Make your own unique zipper pulls.

What You'll Need: Colored leather cords, wild colored shoelaces, lanyard lacings, or satin cords; big beads; jacket, backpack, or purse zipper

Choose the color, pattern, and type of cords or laces according to how you plan to use the zipper pulls. Mixing colors creates cool effects and makes learning this process easier. Start with 2 laces, 1 of each color, about 12 inches long. Thread the 2 laces through the zipper's pull and fold the laces in half so the bottoms are even. You now have 4 laces to work with. Arrange the light-colored laces in the middle and the dark ones on the outside. The lighter laces will always hang straight down the middle. With the 2 dark laces, make a simple knot in front of the lighter laces. Pull tightly. Now use the dark laces to tie a simple knot behind the lighter laces. Pull tightly, and continue knotting above and behind the light-colored laces until the zipper pull is as long as you want it. Thread a large bead on the end of the laces and tie them off.

Make an easy variation by using a metal spring clip or a key ring. Use the same instructions for Zipper Chic, only thread the laces through the swivel base of the metal clip instead. Now slip your metal key ring onto the swivel base of the spring clip. Clip your keys onto your belt loop and voilà! Funky, cool keys to go.

OUCH!

Ever caught a little chin skin in your jacket zipper? Try squirting a little mineral oil into the teeth of the zipper the next time it happens, to help loosen the grip.

CATCH ME IF YOU CAN!

We can't leave out our feline friends! These toys are fun to make and a riot for Fluffy to play with.

What You'll Need: Solid-color or multicolored scrap yarn, medium-size crochet hook, scissors, cardboard

Curl 1 end of the yarn over itself to form a circle. Hold the circle closed with your thumb and index finger. Push part of the long end of the yarn through the circle with your thumb. Pull the loop that is created through the circle with your other hand. Pull tightly so that you form a closed loop. You just made a slipknot! The slipknot will have a short and a long end. Stick the curved part of the crochet hook through the slip knot. Pull the slip knot almost closed around the hook. Wrap the long end of the yarn twice around the index finger of your other hand. Hold the short end of the yarn with the thumb and middle finger of the same hand.

With the curved part of the hook, grab a piece of yarn from your index finger and pull it through the slip knot on the crochet hook. Pull slightly so that you form a closed loop. You've made the first link in the chain! Continue making links in the chain until the chain is about 3 feet long. Make a pom-pom by wrapping some yarn around a 2-inch piece of cardboard about 50 times. Pinch the middle of the yarn, and pull it off the cardboard. With the yarn still held flat between your fingers, knot a piece of yarn tightly around the middle. Snip open the "loop" on either side of the middle. Fluff and trim the ends of the pom-pom, but don't trim the long ends of the yarn you used to tie off the middle. Use the long ends to attach the pom-pom to the end of the chain. Twitch the toy left and right, just out of reach of your feline friend. "Here, kitty, kitty, catch me if you can!"

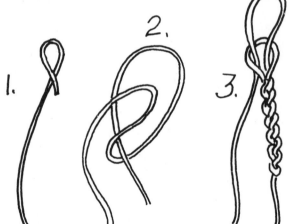

PAPER MAGIC BEADS

7

Paper makes gorgeous beads!

What You'll Need: Gift wrap or Sunday comics, ruler, pencil, scissors, clear gel glue, water, teaspoon, small margarine tub, narrow drinking straws, string or embroidery floss

Use whatever decorative paper you choose. On the backside of the paper, use the ruler and pencil to draw triangles that are 1 inch across the bottom and 7 inches tall. Make as many triangles as you want beads, then cut out the triangles. Mix 2 teaspoons of clear gel glue with 1 teaspoon of water in the small margarine tub. Dip a triangle in the glue mixture, and let the excess glue drip off. Wrap the triangle around a straw, pattern side up, starting with the wide end, to make a rolled bead. Wrap all the triangles, and let them dry for a day. Remove the straw, and string your Paper Magic Beads to make a necklace!

8

BUTTON BONANZA

String together colorful buttons to make your own original jewelry. Shorten the necklace if you'd rather make a bracelet.

What You'll Need: Crazy-color buttons with large holes (try a grab bag from the fabric or craft store), leather cords or shoelaces, scissors

Make sure you have enough buttons and cords or shoelaces to make a necklace of the desired length. Tie a knot at the end of the leather cord or shoelace. With the first button face up, thread the cord up through 1 hole and down through the other. Tie a knot after it. Add more buttons in alternating colors and sizes. They can be placed next to each other or spaced apart with knots in between. If your buttons have 4 holes instead of 2, use double laces. At the end of the cord, make a loop large enough to fit over the first button and tie it off. Model your new necklace!

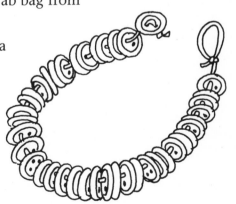

 # PENCIL CUP POSSIBILITIES

9

Jazzing up your room will take the boredom out of homework. Try making other items for a desk set.

What You'll Need: Newspaper; tin can or old coffee mug; poster paints (optional); colorful pictures cut from magazines, old calendars, greeting cards, gift wrap, etc.; scissors; old margarine tub; clear gel glue; water; tablespoon; paintbrush; clear, nontoxic acrylic gloss; yarn or ribbon; rubber stamps and ink pads; glitter glue or glitter marker

Spread the newspaper first! Paint a background color on the can or mug, if desired. While waiting for the paint to dry, cut out pictures you want to put on the container. In an old margarine tub, mix 1 tablespoon of water with 2 tablespoons of clear gel glue. Brush the back of the picture and the spot where the picture is to be placed on the can. Place the picture, then carefully brush a layer of glue over the top. Finish putting on all your cool pictures. Welcome to decoupage! Let the pictures dry for a day. Then coat the pencil cup with clear, nontoxic acrylic gloss, according to directions. (You may need an adult's help with this part.) Glue on extras, such as yarn or ribbon, or adorn with paint, rubber stamps, glitter glue, or glitter marker. Let dry for another day.

Make a power-banking variation. Power to the pennies! (Everything counts, you know.) Use an old piggy bank from a garage sale or another unusual container that can be easily opened. Follow the same decoupage directions as above. Make sure to leave an opening for the cash and for necessary withdrawals!

10 CATCHING RAYS

Recycle old yogurt lids to make dazzling stained-glass sun catchers.

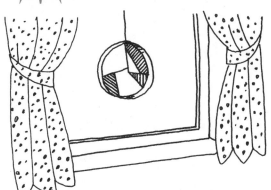

What You'll Need: White paper, permanent markers in several colors including black, yogurt lid with clear plastic "window," tape, gold thread

Practice drawing a simple geometric design on white paper. Make thick, black lines around large, simple areas. Fill the areas with color. When you create a design you like, copy the black lines onto the yogurt lid. Then fill in the blank areas with colored markers. Tape a loop of gold thread to the lip of the lid. Hang your sun catcher!

BIRD CONDO

Build a high-class, high-rise condominium for your feathered friends outdoors.

What You'll Need: Plastic ½-gallon milk or orange juice container with handle, scissors, craft stick or small dowel, newspaper, sphagnum moss, wire coat hanger

Wash the container thoroughly with hot, soapy water. Let dry. On the opposite side from the handle, about halfway down, cut a circular hole about 2 inches wide. Half an inch below the hole, poke the craft stick or small dowel about 1½ inches into the container. This is the bird's perch. Spread out the newspaper, and stuff the sphagnum moss into the bottle until it comes up to the entry hole. Birds like dryer lint, too! Then untwist the coat hanger, and wire the birdhouse, through the handle, to a tree limb not too close to the trunk. (You may need an adult's help to do this part.) Wire it tight enough so that the house doesn't sway too much in the wind. Wait for your bird friends to move in!

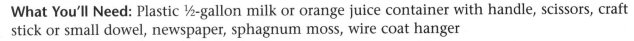

THINGS ON SPRINGS

12

Anybody can make a mobile, but can they make one as springy as yours?

What You'll Need: Coat hanger; brightly colored electrical tape; 4 to 6 little trinkets, game pieces, etc.; construction paper; scissors; black darning thread; needle

Wrap the coat hanger in brightly colored electrical tape. Choose 4 to 6 trinkets to hang from the mobile. Now make large and small "springs." Start by cutting a 3-inch-wide square out of construction paper. Take the square and begin cutting from the outside edge, turning at the corners, and spiraling inward to the center. Leave a "knob" the size of a penny in the center.

Thread the needle, make a knot, and poke through the underside of the "knob." Cut the thread about 5 inches from the knot, and tie the end around the bottom part of the coat hanger. Knot another piece of thread, and, going from the top of the spring to the bottom, poke the needle through the outside edge of the square. Next, knot the thread around a hanging trinket. Notice how the square looks like a spring? Make springs unique by starting with triangular or other shapes and cutting toward the center. To make a longer spring, start with a bigger shape. Use a smaller shape for a shorter spring. Finish making springs and hanging trinkets. Display your springy mobile!

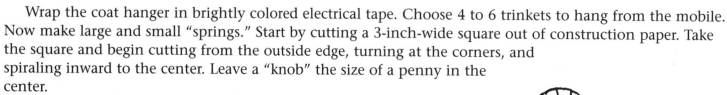

GLITTER GLOBE

13

Snow globes are fun to watch, but these miniature glitter globes are fascinating.

What You'll Need: Small baby food jar, acrylic paint and paintbrush (optional), play dough, any small metal or plastic trinket, iridescent confetti flakes, teaspoon, water

Remove labels from the baby food jar. Wash and dry the jar thoroughly. If you wish, you may paint the outside of the lid with acrylic paints. Let the paint dry. Then put a dime-size amount of clay on the inside of the jar lid, and stick the bottom of the trinket into the clay. Place 1 teaspoon of confetti in the jar; use more or less confetti depending on the size of the jar. Slowly let water trickle into the jar until it's full. Screw the lid on tightly, and turn over the jar. Watch the sparkling glitter rain down!

MAGNETIC FRIDGE FACES

14

This is a fun way to liven up the fridge with duplicate photos.

What You'll Need: Pictures of your family and friends, glue, empty cereal box, scissors, clear adhesive vinyl, small magnet strips

Glue photos to the backside of an unfolded, empty cereal box. Let dry. Then cut photos or tightly trimmed images of people out of the cardboard. Cover the fronts and backs of the photos with clear adhesive vinyl. Glue magnet strips to the backs of the photos. Make a whole set of your friends or family members, and arrange them in wacky ways. You could make separate, goofy speech balloons for everyone, too. This could make a nice gift for your grandparents.

STAINED GLASS VASE

Hate to throw away those neat-looking glass bottles that hold water or iced tea? Make beautiful vases with them!

What You'll Need: Glass bottle with a nice shape, newspaper, clear gel glue, water, tablespoon, old margarine tub, several light-colored shades of tissue paper, paintbrush, clear nontoxic acrylic gloss

Remove all the labels and metal rings from the bottle. Wash and dry it thoroughly. Spread out the newspapers. In the margarine tub, mix 2 tablespoons clear gel glue with 1 tablespoon water. Tear off pieces of tissue paper about the size of a quarter. Work with small areas—brush some glue on the bottle in a patch the size of a quarter. Lay a piece of tissue paper on that part of the bottle. Now hold the piece down with a thumb while lightly brushing glue on top of the paper. Add a piece at time, slightly overlapping the edges. Work carefully! You're only going to do 1 layer. Fold some tissue paper over the lip of the bottle all the way around. Finish covering the bottle. Layer pieces under the bottom edge of the bottle, too. Let dry for a day. Coat the bottle with clear acrylic gloss, according to package directions. Let dry. Add some flowers, and admire what a sunlit window does for your vase!

BOLO TIE

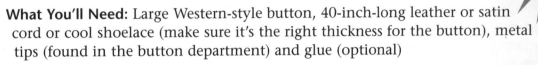

Both guys and gals can wear this easy, Western-style necklace.

What You'll Need: Large Western-style button, 40-inch-long leather or satin cord or cool shoelace (make sure it's the right thickness for the button), metal tips (found in the button department) and glue (optional)

If your favorite button has 2 holes, thread both ends of the cord up through 1 hole and down through the other. If the button has 4 holes, thread 1 end up through 1 hole and down through the other. Then thread the other end of the cord up and down through the hole alongside the first. Glue the metal tips to the ends of the cords, or just tie a knot at each end. Then take your bolo tie two-stepping!

FINDERS, KEEPERS!

When artists find something at a garage sale or lying around the house and use it in sculpture or jewelry, they call it a "found" object. You, too, can search for a vintage doodad for your one-of-a-kind object d'art.

What You'll Need: Newspapers; an unusual, distinctive thing to hang from a necklace (such as an old key, earring, natural stone, game piece, etc.); poster paint and paint-brush or brightly colored nail polish (optional); 36-inch-long black satin cord; scissors

Spread out newspapers, and paint your object if you wish. Make sure you have good ventilation if you are using nail polish. Let the object dry for a day. Fold the satin cord in half to find the center. Wrap the folded center loop around the object and pull the loose ends through the loop. Or tie the object in the center if necessary. Knot the ends of the cord around your neck (be sure the cord is long enough to slip over your head). Then go knock 'em out with your unique sense of style!

FLOWER POWER

Should we say "Power to the Flowers"? The following daisy pattern looks cool when made up into bracelets, necklaces, and earrings. Practicing first with a leather cord and wooden beads is pretty easy and makes chunky, funky jewelry. Once you've got it down, try it with nylon thread and small beads for a delicate look.

What You'll Need: Bracelet: Leather or satin cord (nylon thread), wooden or other bigger-size beads in 3 colors, scissors, matching button, needle (if making the smaller kind of bracelet). Earrings: 2 French wire earrings

Daisy Bracelet: Choose a bead color for flower petals, another color for flower centers, and a third for connecting beads (the connecting beads may be smaller than the others). Tie a knot at the end of the cord, thread on a matching button, and tie another knot after it. Thread on 2 connecting beads. Then add 6 flower petal beads, and thread the cord back up through the first petal bead. Now you have a circle. Thread on a flower center bead. Going toward the left, skip 2 beads and thread the loose end of the cord through the third bead. Pull tight. The first "daisy" is made. Add 2 connecting beads, make another daisy, and continue until the bracelet is the right length for your wrist. At the end, add connecting beads to make a loop big enough to slip over the button. Note: If you're making the daintier kind of bracelet, use 8 connecting beads between flowers. Also, use 8 beads to make the daisies and skip 3 beads before threading the loose end of the nylon thread through the fourth bead.

Flower Necklace: Use a matching button if you're making a choker. If you're making a longer necklace, skip the button and make a knot 3 inches from the end of the cord. Follow Daisy Bracelet instructions above. Tie the ends of the necklace together (be sure it is long enough to slip over your head).

Daisy Earrings: Use French wire earrings from the craft store in addition to the other supplies listed above. Make a knot at the end of the cord. Use a matching color of thread to attach the French wires to the cord between the knot and the connecting beads. Thread on 4 or 5 connecting beads, depending on the length you want. Make a daisy according to the Daisy Bracelet instructions above. Tie off. Note: If you're using small beads, thread on 8 to 10 connecting beads. Make 3 daisies, with 2 to 4 connecting beads between flowers. Then thread the needle through the last connecting bead before the first daisy and pull tight, making a mini loop. Tie off.

KITTY'S FAVORITE MOUSE

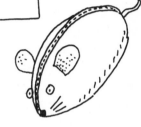

19

Your cat may like this mouse so much that you'll have to keep more than one mouse in the house!

What You'll Need: Scrap paper, felt scraps, scissors, yarn, yarn needle, black marker, catnip

On the paper, draw a small hill shape about 2 inches high and 2 inches wide, with a straight line at the bottom. Cut it out, and use it as a pattern to cut out 2 pieces of felt. Match up the 2 pieces of felt and stitch them together around the outside top curve. Stuff the mouse with catnip until it's plump. Stitch the bottom edge closed. Draw in the eyes, one on either side of the seam. Cut out 2 circles of felt that are 1 inch wide. These are the ears. Sew them on, just above and slightly to the side of each eye. Use a few tight stitches on part of the ear nearest the eye. Let the other side remain loose. Draw on a nose and whiskers with the marker.

Sew a yarn tail on the other end.

Pattern

20

NO, NO, FIDO!

Here's one for doggie's owner. Dogs don't like the noise a shaker can makes. They will stop misbehaving if you shake the can whenever you catch them in the act.

What You'll Need: Clean, empty diet shake can; 5 pennies; clear packing tape; white paper; ruler; scissors; markers; clear tape

Put the pennies in the can. Cover the top of the can with clear packing tape. Cut a 9×4½-inch label out of white paper . Decorate the label with markers. Tape one end of the label to the can. Make small rolls of tape, and stick them between the label and the can. Overlap the other end of the label over the first end and tape it down.

SCOTTY BISCOTTI

21

Pets really appreciate gifts—especially edible ones! Try out these gourmet doggie biscuits on your favorite pooch.

What You'll Need: 1½ cups cornmeal, 1¾ cups flour, ½ cup powdered milk, 1 teaspoon baking soda, 1 teaspoon salt, 2 finely crumbled beef bouillon cubes dissolved in ¼ cup hot water, 3 eggs, 2 finely crumbled chicken bouillon cubes dissolved in ¼ cup hot water, measuring cups and spoons, 2 mixing bowls, sifter, mixer, cookie sheet, waxed paper, cutting board, knife, airtight container

Have an adult help you with the oven. Preheat the oven to 300 degrees. Wash your hand before making this recipe (and when you are finished). Combine the dry ingredients, and sift them twice into a large bowl. In a separate bowl, combine the liquid ingredients. Slowly add the liquid ingredients to the dry ones with a mixer. When the mixture is "doughy," divide it into 2 flat, oval loaves about 12 inches long. Line a cookie sheet with a layer of waxed paper. Transfer the loaves to the cookie sheet. (You can shape the sides to look like dog biscuits if you like.) Bake for about 50 minutes or until the loaves are almost firm to the touch. Remove from the oven, and cool for 10 minutes.

On a cutting board, cut the loaves into ½-inch slices. Lay the slices on the cookie sheet and bake for 25 minutes. Then turn the slices over with a pancake turner and bake for another 25 minutes. Turn the oven off, and let the biscotti cool in the oven with the door propped open a little. The slices will be hard and crunchy—just what canines love. Serve your Scotty Biscotti and experience doggie devotion! These can be stored in an airtight container for 2 weeks.

DOGGIE FACTS
Have a question about your puppy? Turn to Digital Dog at
http://www.digitaldog.com. This Internet stop will keep you
barking up the right tree.

MAGICAL MOSAIC PUZZLE PICTURE

Recycle an old puzzle by painting a picture on it. Play with it or frame it!

What You'll Need: Newspaper; old shirt; discarded puzzle, either 8×10 or 10×17 in size; opaque white and other colors of poster paint; paintbrush; pencil; frame for framing or box for storing puzzle

This is messy but worth it! Spread out the newspaper, and throw on an old shirt. Assemble the puzzle on the newspaper. Paint the entire surface of the puzzle with the white paint. Let dry. If you can see any of the original picture underneath, paint on another coat of white and let dry. If necessary, add a third coat and let dry for a few hours. While the paint is drying, plan what you are going to paint on the puzzle. You could make an original picture or copy one of your favorite drawings. Lightly sketch the picture on the puzzle with the pencil. Get out the other colors of paint and paint away. Let the paint dry overnight. Your puzzle picture is ready for playing with or framing!

CONE CREATURES

What kind of creatures do you like? Martians? Purple People Eaters? Make them all!

What You'll Need: Table covering, smock, pinecones of various sizes, cotton balls, poster paint, paintbrushes, yarn, chenille stems, fabric scraps, white glue, wiggle eyes, glitter glue

Cover the table and put on a smock or old shirt before beginning this project. Fill out your pinecone creatures with cotton balls. Paint them any color you like and let dry. Adorn them with yarn for hair, chenille stems for limbs, and fabric scraps for clothes. Don't forget to glue on those wiggle eyes. Top off with touches of glitter glue and let dry. Oh no—it's the attack of the cone creatures! Better go make some more!

PAPER CARNATIONS

Every vase needs flowers! And these tissue-paper beauties will be perfect for your stained glass vase (see project 15).

What You'll Need: Brightly colored tissue paper, ruler, dull pencil, scissors, green chenille stems, clear tape, green florist tape

Using 3 layers of 1 color of tissue paper, cut out a section about 12 inches long and 3 inches wide (see illustration). In the lower left-hand and right-hand corners, make a pencil mark ½ inch above the bottom edge. Now carefully draw a straight line across the tissue from pencil mark to pencil mark. Also in the lower left-hand corner, make a second mark ½ inch above the line. From the second mark, draw a diagonal line to the top right corner. Cut off the excess tissue paper above the diagonal line. All the way across the tissue paper, make narrow cuts from the top diagonal edge down to the straight line across the bottom.

Place the top part of the chenille stem in the corner of the short end, and tape it down. Roll the pipe cleaner toward the long end. Make sure the bottom edges of the tissue paper always line up. When done, tape the bottom edge of the tissue paper down. Wrap green florist tape around the top of the chenille stem and 1 inch up the flower. Now slowly pull down and fluff out the flower "petals," working from the outside in toward the center. Behold your carnation! Experiment with other color combinations and shapes of petals to make other kinds of flowers.

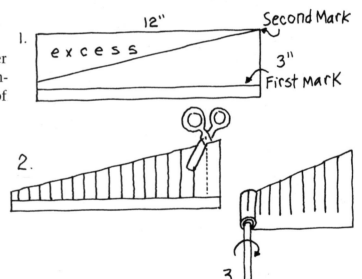

CINNAMON "SCENT"-SATIONS

These beads not only look good, they smell good, too!

What You'll Need: Lots of cinnamon and applesauce, measuring cup, bowl, mixing spoon, aluminum foil (not plastic wrap), toothpick, tiny cookie cutters (optional), wire rack, pointed knife, rolling pin, string or embroidery floss

Mix ¼ cup (really!) cinnamon and ¼ cup applesauce. This makes a small batch to experiment with. Lay a sheet of foil on the counter. Put the cinnamon clay on the foil and cover the clay with another sheet of foil. (This keeps your hands from getting stained.) Roll the clay out into a "snake" about a ½ inch thick. Cut the beads to the desired length. Shape them in rounds, squares, cylinders, etc. Use the toothpick to put a hole through each bead. Make sure the hole is wide enough at both ends for the string you will use. Let the beads dry for a day or so on a wire rack. For a variation, you can roll the cinnamon clay out in a sheet and use tiny cookie cutters or a pointed knife to carve out flat, shaped beads. Very carefully stick a toothpick through the flat beads to make the holes.

DOUGH BEADS

You'll have all the fun with these beads and none of the mess of mixing flour and food coloring.

What You'll Need: Different colors of play dough, toothpicks, tiny cookie cutters, rolling pin, waxed paper, string or embroidery floss

Roll the dough out ¼ inch to ½ inch thick for round beads and about ¼ inch thick for flat shapes. Use cookie cutters to cut out flat beads. Use a toothpick to carve small details into the beads and to make holes. Make sure the holes are equally wide at both ends and also big enough for whatever string you will use. To make a very cool-looking marbled bead, mix 2 colors thoroughly. (Adding shapes of another color on top won't work, because they will fall apart when dry.) Let your beads dry for a day or 2 on waxed paper until hard. Then string up your colorful creations.

TIN CAN LUMINARIES

27

Your lights will twinkle brightly in these luminaries. The designs are made by tapping holes into a tin can with a hammer and a large nail.

What You'll Need: Clean tin cans with labels removed and only 1 end opened, dark-colored crayon, water, large nail, hammer, metallic copper acrylic paint, paintbrushes, tea candles

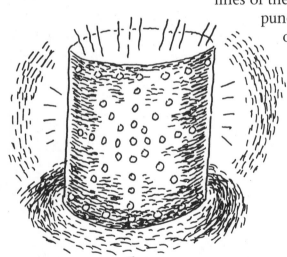

Decide on a simple outline or drawing to use. Using the crayon, draw the design in the middle of each side of the can. You can also draw a straight line around the bottom and the top for a border. Fill the can with water and set upright in the freezer. Wait for the water to freeze solid. Take the can outside and stand on a concrete stoop or sidewalk. (Have an adult help you with this part.) Lay the can on the ground between your feet to hold it in place. Following your crayon pattern on the can, carefully tap holes into the lines of the design by placing the point of the nail along the line and punching it through with the hammer. Continue hammering along outline, and make the holes about a ¼ inch apart. When you are done, dump the ice out. Dry the can, and then let it air dry for an hour or so. Then paint only the outside of the can—try a metallic copper color. Drop in a tea candle, and admire the glow.

THAT'S SOME CAN

In 1939, a tin can of roast veal and gravy was found from Sir Edward Perry's 1824 voyage in search of the Northwest Passage. The can was opened, and the contents were still nutritious—even after more than 100 years!

CREATIVE CARDS

These greeting cards are cool to make and even better to give away. And they make great displays because they stand up on their own!

What You'll Need: Empty cereal box, scissors, old greeting card, white paper, pencil, solid-color and coordinating patterned gift wrap that fits the theme of the occasion, glue, scrap paper, markers, glitter glue, ink pads, rubber stamps

Cut and unfold an empty cereal box. Open the greeting card and lay it flat on a piece of white paper. Trace around the greeting card, and cut out the shape. Use the tracing as a pattern to cut out 1 piece each of the cereal box cardboard and the solid-color gift wrap. Fold the cardboard in half, with the printed side on the outside. Glue the solid-color gift wrap to the printed side of the cardboard. Practice writing out the message for the front and the inside on a scrap of paper. Using markers, copy your message onto the front of the card. Fold the white paper in half. Then write the inside message on the inside of the white paper. Glue the white paper to the gray side of the cardboard. Cut out big and small pictures from the patterned gift wrap. Glue them on the front and the inside of the card. Finish decorating the card with glitter glue and rubber stamps and ink pads. Admire your handiwork, then give it away!

FOREVER FRIENDS

29

Is anybody else at your school wearing a velvety friendship bracelet? All it takes is five minutes to start a trend!

What You'll Need: 3 different colors of thick, chunky-weight chenille yarn, scissors, ruler, masking tape, 2 large wooden or plastic beads

Make bright friendship bracelets using 3 strands of yarn that are 9 inches long each. Line up the strands and knot them; leave 1 inch free at the end. Tape the end to a table edge, then thread a large bead next to the knot. Braid the yarn down to 1 inch from the end. Thread on the other large bead. Tie an end knot after the bead. Wrap your cool bracelet around your wrist, and push the beads through the braids on the opposite sides, or simply tie the ends off. Make plenty of bracelets for your friends, too.

STORY CHARACTERS

Re-create your favorite hero or heroine from science fiction stories or fairy tales! Use them for play-time or as decorations.

What You'll Need: Several colors of play dough, toothpicks

Choose your favorite characters and mold them out of play dough. Attach body parts by using toothpicks. Stick a toothpick or part of a toothpick into the top of the body. Then slide the head onto the other end of the toothpick. (Be careful to keep the toothpicks away from younger brothers and sisters. Let them have their own play dough to play with.) Two colors can be mashed together to form a neat, marbled color. Unfortunately, adding 1 shape on top of another without toothpicks won't work; the shapes will fall apart when dry. Let your characters dry for 2 or 3 days. Now use your desktop for a stage and act out your favorite story!

TOO BEAUTIFUL TO USE

According to an article in *Smithsonian Magazine*, toothpicks were once valuable items, often made of gold, silver, or ivory, and they were often encrusted with gems. When Princess Louise Marie Therese of Parma married a prince of Austria, her dowry included 12 such toothpicks.

PICTURE THIS

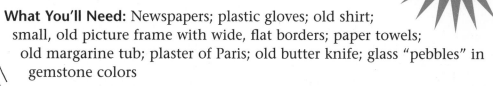

Turn discarded frames into jeweled masterpieces.

What You'll Need: Newspapers; plastic gloves; old shirt; small, old picture frame with wide, flat borders; paper towels; old margarine tub; plaster of Paris; old butter knife; glass "pebbles" in gemstone colors

Spread out the newspapers, and put on your gloves and an old shirt. Ask an adult to remove any glass from the frame and set it in a safe place. Wipe off the frame with a damp paper towel, then dry it off. In the margarine tub, mix a small amount of the plaster of Paris according to package directions. (Have an adult help you with this part.) Use an old knife to spread plaster on the picture frame. Place a row of glass pebbles around the inner edge of the frame. Make sure the pebbles are evenly spaced and in a variety of colors! Finish covering the frame surface in rows of "jewels." Let dry for a day. Use the leftover plaster to bejewel a flowerpot or throw it away in the trash, but don't pour it down the sink—it could cause a nasty clog! Enjoy your "jewel" of a frame!

TREASURE BOX

When you're done, the box will look like a treasure all by itself!

What You'll Need: Uncooked pasta (wagon wheels, cartoon characters, other shapes), cardboard school supply box, yarn, white glue, gold acrylic paint, paintbrush, glitter markers

Play with the pasta shapes on the box, and come up with combinations that form interesting patterns or pictures. Do the same with pieces of yarn. Next, glue the yarn and pasta shapes on the box. Let the box dry for a day. Then paint the box gold with the acrylic paint. Let dry for a few hours. Finally, add surface details with glitter markers in contrasting colors. Fill that sparkly box with treasures!

YOU'RE A STAR

33

Show someone they're appreciated or reward them for a special deed.

What You'll Need: Flour, salt, cream of tartar, water, cooking oil, measuring cups and spoons, saucepan, mixing spoon, waxed paper, rolling pin, cookie cutters, pencil or straw, wire cooling rack, poster paints, paintbrush, glitter markers, ribbons

Have an adult help you make the clay. To mix up a small batch of play clay, stir together 2 cups of flour, ½ cup of salt, and 2 tablespoons of cream of tartar in a saucepan. Then add 1 cup of water and 2 tablespoons of cooking oil. Put the pan over medium heat, and cook for 3 to 5 minutes. Stir the mixture constantly until it looks like mashed potatoes. Dump the clay out on a sheet of waxed paper, but wait until the clay is cool enough to touch. Roll out the play clay to a layer about ¼ inch thick. Cut out stars (or other appropriate shapes) with cookie cutters. With a pencil or straw, make a hole in the top, but not too close to the edge. The size of the hole depends on the thickness of the ribbon you're using. Let the cutouts air dry for 24 hours on a wire rack. Paint them with poster paints, and let dry. With the glitter markers, write on the names of the people who are receiving your awards and add any other messages. Thread ribbons through the holes and present your awards!

BLUE RIBBON WINNERS

We've all heard of the Academy Awards and the Emmies. But what awards do most Americans receive? Simple blue, red, and yellow ribbons, according to experts at Delta Awards in California.

"PIN"-DEMONIUM

34

Make one for each of your friends! Have fun collecting each other's artworks.

What You'll Need: Diaper pins with animal faces or large safety pins, brightly colored nail polish (optional), newspaper, clear nail polish, small beads that fit the open shaft of the safety pin, clear gel glue, colored ribbons

If you don't have diaper pins with animal faces, paint large safety pins a bright color of nail polish. Spread out newspaper when painting. (Make sure you have good ventilation.) Let the polish dry completely, then turn pins over and paint the other side. It will take 3 or 4 coats, depending on the thickness of the polish. Let the pins dry between each coat. Next, give the pins 2 coats of clear polish and let dry. Thread the beads onto the lower, open pin shafts. Make sure to leave enough room to close the safety pins. Now spread clear gel glue over the beads with your fingers, making sure some glue gets between all the beads. Let pins dry for a few hours. Add a second coat of glue and let dry again. Tie coordinating ribbon through the hole at the bottom of the pin.

BOOK LOOKS

35

Make your history book even more exciting with color!

What You'll Need: Textbooks; large white paper; pencil; Sunday comics, recycled gift wrap, or your own drawings; scissors; clear adhesive vinyl; clear tape

Lay the open book on the white paper. Trace around the edges of the book with the pencil, allowing for flaps 2 inches deep all the way around the book. Cut out your pattern. Place the pattern on the gift wrap or other decorative paper. Trace around the pattern and cut out. Peel the backing off a piece of adhesive vinyl that is bigger than the cover. Starting with one end, carefully lay the adhesive vinyl, sticky side down, on the front of the decorative paper. Smooth it out as you go. Cut off the excess adhesive vinyl. Lay the cover face down on the table, and center the book on the cover. Mark, with a black dot, where the corners hit the cover. Cut slits on either side of the spine and tuck those flaps inside the spine. Line up the corners of the front cover of the book with the dots. Fold in the corners first, then fold in the 2-inch side flaps. Repeat for the back cover. Tape the flaps to each other, not the book.

SNAZZY SCRAPBOOK

36

Share happy memories with someone, or showcase their awesome vacation souvenirs.

What You'll Need: 5×7-inch autograph book or journal with unlined pages, white paper, pencil, scissors, ½ yard of fake fur or other novelty fabric, white glue, solid-color paper, different colors of felt, fancy scissors that cut in patterns, glitter and regular markers, glitter glue, multicolored glue, ink pad, ink stamps

Plan a theme for the scrapbook, and choose your supplies accordingly. Open the autograph book, and lay it flat on white paper. Trace around the book (add about ¼ inch to one side—you can trim the fabric later if it is too big) and cut out. Use the white paper as a pattern to cut out the novelty fabric. Stand the book up with its pages open. Coat the front and back covers and spine with white glue. Smear a thin coat of white glue on the backside of the fabric. Line up the corners of one side of the book with the backside of the fabric. Press down with a clean hand inside the book. Close the book, press the fabric around the spine and into the grooves, and then press the second side down. Let dry for a day. Trim fabric if needed.

Meanwhile, using the colored paper, cut out background circles, squares, triangles, etc., for photos or other mementos with the fancy scissors. Decide how you will place them inside the book. Cut out other shapes from felt. Play around with the contents of the book until you're satisfied. Glue everything down with white glue. Decorate the inside and cover of the scrapbook with markers, glitter glue, multicolored glue, and ink stamps.

TAKING BETTER PICTURES

To take a good picture, remember to have a "strong center of interest," according to Kodak's Web site (found at http://Kodak.com). A picture can only tell one story at a time—make sure your picture tells the story you want it to! Check out other picture-taking tips from Kodak at their Web site.

CELEBRATE LIFE

Celebrations are natural to people the world over. People in every culture honor days of personal importance, the changing seasons, cultural achievements, religious traditions, and more. The holidays may be different from place to place, but what is common is the joy of celebrating life. By learning about the holidays and traditions of different cultures you can learn something about the people of those cultures. You will discover how they are unique and different from you, and also how they are very much the same!

HANUKKAH MENORAH

37

Build a menorah for Hanukkah, the Jewish Festival of Lights.

What You'll Need: 2 cups flour, 1 cup salt, 1½ cups water, spoon, bowl, paint, paintbrush

To make your menorah, mix a batch of baker's clay by mixing the flour and salt in the bowl. Add the water and mix. Form the dough into a ball, and knead it for 5 minutes. Now it is ready for molding. Make 9 candle cups by either molding the dough or rolling it out and coiling it around to make a small cup. You will need 8 cups for the 8 nights of Hanukkah and a ninth cup for the special candle that is used to light the other candles. Make a base out of the dough and attach the candle cups to the base. Place 8 cups in a row and then set the ninth cup higher up and off to the side or in the middle just behind the others. The candleholder can be set to dry for a few days or baked at 300 degrees until hard. Once it's hard, paint it to express how wonderful you feel about this holiday!

HARVEST PLACEMATS

38

Create decorative placemats that symbolize harvest time.

What You'll Need: Onion, apple, mushroom, garlic clove, brussels sprout, cabbage wedge, and/or other fruits and vegetables; knife; table covering; clean foam food trays; paint; construction paper; clear adhesive vinyl

These festive mealtime decorations can be used to celebrate any of the many international harvest festivals. Make the harvest placemats by printing with fruit and vegetables. Choose several fruits or vegetables and cut each in half. (Have an adult help you with the cutting.) Cover the table. Pour several colors of paint into clean foam food trays. Choose fall colors or create your own personal color scheme. Dip the cut side of the fruit or vegetable into the paint, and then make a print on a sheet of construction paper. Make several prints on the paper. You can cover each sheet of paper with a combination of fruit and vegetable prints or a single fruit printed with different colors. Let the paint dry, and then seal the placemats in clear adhesive vinyl. To seal, cut 2 pieces of clear adhesive vinyl slightly larger than the construction paper placemat. Peel the white paper off a sheet, and place the adhesive vinyl on a table, sticky side up. Carefully lay the placemat on top of the adhesive vinyl, and gently rub it so it sticks. Then peel the white paper off the second sheet of adhesive vinyl, and carefully place it, sticky side down, on top of the unsealed side of the placemat. Gently rub to seal, and trim the edges if necessary. Now the easy-to-clean placemats are ready for a holiday meal!

WOVEN KWANZA MAT

39

Make a mkeka, one of the seven symbolic items of the African American Kwanza festival.

What You'll Need: Black, green, and red construction paper; scissors; ruler; tape

The mkeka (a woven mat) is the Kwanza symbol of history. To weave a mkeka, cut parallel lines in a piece of black construction paper. Cut the lines starting 1 inch from the bottom edge to 1 inch from the top edge. To make cutting easier, fold the paper in half and cut starting from the middle going toward the edge. Unfold your black "loom," and cut strips of red and green paper for weaving. Weave the strips of paper in and out of the black loom, alternating red and green strips. After weaving, secure the paper strips in place by taping the back of the mkeka. To make a more decorative mat, you can weave with colored ribbon instead of construction paper.

40

CHRISTMAS POMANDER

Make a fragrant holiday pomander, and fill the air with sweet-smelling spicy cheer.

What You'll Need: Orange, whole cloves, dish, pointed wooden toothpicks, ribbon

Pomanders are made by gathering good-smelling herbs, spices, or other things into a cloth bag or small box, or by studding an apple or orange with spices. Spicy pomanders can be hung in hallways or on Christmas trees, or they can be set on tables for Christmas decorations. (People also use pomanders in drawers or closets to add a good smell to clothing or linens.) Make a scented holiday pomander by inserting whole cloves into an orange. Set the cloves out in a dish so they'll be easier to pick up. Use the toothpicks to make holes in the orange skin. Insert the stick-end of the cloves into the holes. Push each clove in all the way so the clove top sits right on the orange skin. Add cloves until you're happy with the way it looks. Wrap a colorful ribbon twice around the studded orange. Knot the ribbon on the top. Then make a loop with the ribbon ends so the pomander can be hung. (You can also use a lemon for the pomander.)

HARVEST CORN DOLL

41

Cornhusk dolls have been traditional autumn ornaments in England for hundreds of years. Introduce the tradition to your family!

What You'll Need: Cornhusks, bowl of water, yarn, scissors, permanent marker, glue, fabric scraps (optional)

Make a cornhusk doll for decoration or for play. These dolls were first made in ancient England to celebrate harvest time. To make your own cornhusk doll, carefully peel the husks off 2 ears of corn. Place the husks in a bowl of water, and soak them until they soften. Remove them from the water, but allow them to remain damp. Start to make your doll by rolling a cornhusk into a ball for the doll's head. Layer 4 more cornhusks, and fold them over the head. Tie a piece of yarn under the head. Layer 2 more cornhusks, and roll them together lengthwise. Slip these under the head to create arms. Tie yarn at each end to make hands. Tie another piece of yarn under the arms to secure them in place and to make the doll's waist. Cut the ends of the husks hanging below the doll's waist to make legs. Tie yarn near the bottom of each leg to make feet. When the husks are dry, draw a face on the doll using a permanent marker. (Be sure the husks are dry—otherwise the markers might bleed.) Make hair for your doll with yarn, and glue it on. Keep the doll natural in his or her cornhusk clothing, or create a more decorative outfit by cutting out scraps of fabric and gluing them on the doll.

Harvest Festivals

Some holidays that honor harvest time are Thanksgiving in the United States and Canada, Oktoberfest in Germany, Moon Festival in China, and Rice Festival in Japan. Native Americans celebrate Green Corn Festival, Jewish people celebrate Sukkot, and many African Americans celebrate Kwanza.

LUNAR NEW YEAR GARDEN

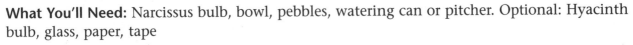

42

Plant a narcissus bulb so that it flowers in time for the Chinese Lunar New Year.

What You'll Need: Narcissus bulb, bowl, pebbles, watering can or pitcher. Optional: Hyacinth bulb, glass, paper, tape

The Chinese New Year is celebrated on the first day of the first lunar month (sometime in January or February). The narcissus is a traditional New Year's flower in China; it symbolizes good luck. Start your New Year's garden 4 to 5 weeks before the lunar new year. To "force" the narcissus to bloom early, put pebbles in a shallow bowl. Set the narcissus bulb in the pebbles with the pointy side up. Place the bulb in a sunny window, and make sure the bulb always has water. Flowers will blossom in 4 to 5 weeks. A hyacinth bulb can also be forced to blossom by setting it in a glass of water, with the pointy side up, so that the bottom is sitting in the water. Make a cone-shaped hat to cover the tip. Keep the bulb in a cool place for 8 weeks, making sure it always has enough water. After 8 weeks, move it to a warm spot and watch it bloom.

43

MOON FESTIVAL MOONCAKES

Make mooncakes to share sweetness and good luck!

What You'll Need: ½ cup butter; ¼ cup sugar; 1 egg yolk; 1 cup flour; ¼ teaspoon salt; jelly or jam; chopped nuts, raisins, or sesame seeds (optional); mixing bowl; measuring cups and spoons; aluminum foil; cookie sheet; mixing spoon; cooling racks; spatula

The Moon Festival is celebrated in China in September when the moon is full. The holiday, a tribute to the moon, is also a time to celebrate the harvest. Mooncakes are a traditional part of the festivities, which are believed by some to honor the moon's birthday! To make mooncakes, first wash your hands. Then mix the butter, sugar, and egg yolk. Stir until the mixture is creamy. Add the flour and salt to the mixture. Stir thoroughly. Form the dough into a ball. Wrap the ball in foil, and refrigerate it for 30 minutes. After the dough has chilled, wash your hands and unwrap the foil. Break off small pieces and form them into mooncakes by rolling small balls (moons). Make a hole in the middle of each mooncake using your finger or thumb. Put a teaspoon of jelly or jam into each hole. (You can also add chopped nuts, raisins, or sesame seeds.) Have an adult help you bake the mooncakes in a preheated oven at 375 degrees for 20 minutes. Then let the cookies cool on racks. Share the mooncakes with a friend to bring good luck!

MINIATURE JAPANESE SAND GARDEN

44

Create a mini replica of an ancient Zen sand garden. These gardens are used in Japan for quiet meditation, as they were hundreds of years ago.

What You'll Need: Box top, sand, rocks and pebbles, small cardboard rectangles, scissors

In a Zen sand garden, the sand and rocks are arranged to represent natural lakes and mountains and to inspire contemplative thinking. To make your own small garden, fill an empty gift box or shoe box top with clean, damp sand. Place a few rocks or pebbles in the garden, either in small clusters or all alone, to stand for hills and mountains. Then make wavy water ripple lines in the sand with a cardboard comb. To make the combs, cut different-size notches in each of several cardboard pieces. Experiment with each notched cardboard piece, combing through the sand to discover the comb's effects. Pat the sand down after combing to try a new comb or to rearrange your design. Comb a pleasing water design around the mountains, and set the sand garden on a table or desk as a decoration or centerpiece to inspire your own quiet thinking!

BALLOON PINATA

45

Make a pinata, a Latin American holiday custom, and turn any occasion into a real party.

What You'll Need: Balloon, newspaper, large bowl, water, flour, paint, paintbrush, yarn, candy and toys (optional), broom handle or bat, blindfold

Pinatas were first made by Mexican Indians long before the Spaniards ever explored the Americas. The Spanish explorers helped popularize the pinata after their arrival by bringing the custom back to Spain and Portugal. Today pinatas are widely used in Mexico and in many other parts of the world as part of holiday celebrations. Colorful pinatas are filled with candy or toys and hung as holiday decorations. Later, children play a pinata game. They gather in a circle around the pinata, and players take turns being blindfolded and striking at the pinata with a stick as the other players sing. When the pinata finally breaks, all the players scramble for the goodies! To make a balloon pinata, tear newspaper into strips. Mix flour and water together to make a paste. Blow up a balloon, and cover it with strips of newspaper dipped in the flour and water paste. Cover the balloon completely. Allow it to dry for a day or 2, turning it occasionally during that time. When the balloon is dry, paint it in bright, decorative colors. Then, with adult help, cut the top off the balloon and punch several holes around the top edge. Thread yarn through the holes, tie them together, and hang up your pinata. Fill the balloon with candy or toys if you want to use it (and break it) for the pinata game!

DANCE THE RAIN DOWN

46

Make a rainmaker shaker and, in the tradition of many Native American and African peoples, dance and play music to invite the skies to rain!

What You'll Need: Cardboard tube; stapler; beans, buttons, or other small objects; paint; paintbrushes

Rainmakers in Uganda shake handmade rattles that sound like rain when they do their rain dance. To make a rainmaker shaker, staple 1 end of a cardboard tube closed. Fill the tube with beans, buttons, or other small objects that will make noise. Then staple the other end to seal the rattle. Paint the tube, and let it dry. When it's dry outside, invent a dance using the rainmaker and invite the sky to bring forth water!

GROUNDHOG DAY SHADOW INVESTIGATION

Never celebrated Groundhog Day? Here's a way to make the day special.

What You'll Need: Stiff paper, ruler, pencil, crayons, scissors, masking tape, flashlight

Celebrate Groundhog Day by investigating shadows with a flashlight and a stand-up groundhog drawing. The traditional tale about this day is that the groundhog wakes from his winter hibernation on February 2 (the midpoint of winter) and comes out of his hole. The groundhog is then supposed to take a peek around. If he sees his shadow, it means there will be 6 more weeks of winter cold. If he does not, warm weather is on the way. Though the tale is popular, it is not scientifically accurate! But you can still take advantage of the holiday to learn something about shadow casting. On a piece of stiff paper, draw a horizontal line about 1½ inches from the bottom for a ground line. Draw a groundhog sitting on the ground line. Color your groundhog, and cut off the excess paper around his outline (but don't cut along the ground line). Fold the bottom of the paper on the ground line so that the bottom becomes a base for a stand-up groundhog. Tape the base to the floor. Darken the room and shine a flashlight at the groundhog from different angles. Notice what happens to the groundhog's shadow as you change the angle and distance of the light you shine on him.

DECORATIVE PAINTED EGGS

48

Paint a portrait, picture, or scene on an egg, and follow in the footsteps of an ancient Chinese tradition.

What You'll Need: Egg, paper clip, container, modeling clay, watercolors, paintbrush, pencil

Before painting the eggshell, remove the egg inside so your painting can last for a long time. To pierce the shell, unbend a paper clip and wash it. Then, carefully make a small opening in the larger end of the egg by gently piercing the shell. Break the egg yolk inside the egg, and mix the egg so the contents will come out. Pour the egg contents out into a small container and discard. Make a modeling clay collar for the eggshell (see project 51), and set the eggshell, broken side down (and hidden!), in the clay collar. The "egg canvas" is ready for painting. Paint a picture on the blank shell using watercolors, or sketch your drawing on the shell with pencil first and then paint.

49

REBUS VALENTINE

Send your Valentine message in rebus writing, and challenge your friends to figure out the meanings of the picture sentences!

What You'll Need: Paper, markers or crayons

First figure out your Valentine message. Rebus writing uses pictures, objects, or symbols that have names that sound like the words you want to express. To write a rebus message, first write your Valentine greeting on scrap paper. Then figure out pictures and letters you can use to come up with the sounds for each word. There are many different ways to represent any word. Use your creativity to come up with fun and original pictures for each word of your message, and then put your friends to the test! For example, "You are the apple of my eye" can be written using a picture of a ewe for the word "you," the letter "R" for the word "are," a picture of an apple for "apple," the letter "M" + a picture of an eye for "my," and a picture of an eye for "eye." "I like you!" can be written: picture of an eye for "I," the letter "L" + a picture of a bike - the letter "B" for "like," and the letter "U" for "you." "Be mine!" can be written: picture of a bee for "be," and the letter "M" + the number "9" - the letter "N" for "mine."

SECRET HEART VALENTINE

50

Shhhh! It's a secret, Valentine.

What You'll Need: Colored paper, ruler, scissors, pencil, glue, marker

Hide a heart in a colorful open-out Valentine card. Cut four paper squares (8×8 inches, 6×6 inches, 4×4 inches, and 1¾×1¾ inches) each in a different color. Cut the smallest square into a heart shape, and set the heart aside. Draw pencil borders from end to end on each side of the 3 larger squares. Make 2-inch borders for the largest square, 1½-inch borders for the middle square, and 1-inch borders for the smallest square. Cut out the corners created on the squares by the intersecting border lines. Cutting out the corners will create a tab on each square side. With scissors, round off the corners of the tabs. Fold the tabs inward along the pencil lines. Using a small drop of glue, paste the smallest square in the middle of the medium square, and the medium square in the middle of the largest square. Glue the heart in the middle of the smallest square, and write a tiny message in it. Now close the smallest square by tucking each of the 4 semi-circular flaps under the other. Close the medium square and then the biggest square in the same way. Your secret hidden heart is ready!

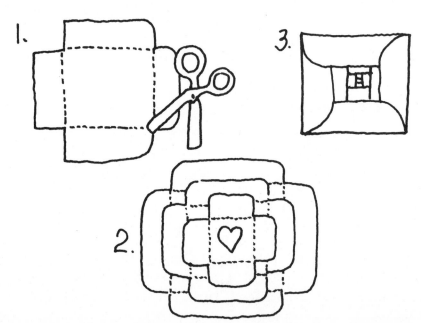

ADORNED EGGS

51

Here are two exciting new ways to decorate Easter eggs.

What You'll Need: Bowls, food coloring, vinegar, cooking oil, water, measuring spoons, hard-boiled eggs, large spoon, paper towels, modeling clay, newspaper, rubber cement

For marbleized egg decorations, mix together in a small mixing bowl: 1 tablespoon food coloring, 1 tablespoon vinegar, and 1 tablespoon cooking oil. Add 2 cups of water, and stir the liquid around quickly until it begins to swirl. Now, using a spoon, quickly dip a hard-boiled egg into the swirling colored liquid and pull it back out again. Pat the egg dry with a paper towel and repeat the procedure, this time dipping the egg into a solution of a different color. For a drizzle-decorated egg, combine ½ cup hot water, ½ tablespoon food coloring, and 1 teaspoon vinegar. Let the solution cool. Meanwhile, make a small collar out of modeling clay to stand the egg in. To make the collar, roll out a snake shape, flatten it, then mold it into a cylinder the egg can sit on. Put the collar on a piece of newspaper. Place the hard-boiled egg on the collar and drizzle it with rubber cement (have an adult help you with the rubber cement, and make sure the room is well ventilated). Let the rubber cement dry. Then, using a spoon, dip the egg into the dye solution. Remove the egg and pat with a paper towel. Set the egg on the collar. When the dye is dry, rub off the rubber cement.

TANGRAM PUZZLE

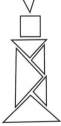

52

Tangram puzzles have been used in China for entertainment and fun since ancient times.

What You'll Need: Tagboard, ruler, scissors, pencil

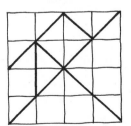

The Chinese call the puzzle *ch'i ch'iao t'u,* which means "ingenious puzzle with seven pieces." Seven geometric shapes make up the puzzle pieces. Rearranged in different ways, these 7 pieces can make as many as 1,600 different designs. To make your own tangram puzzle, cut out an 8×8-inch tagboard square. Using the ruler, draw a grid to create 16 squares. Then, following the diagram, mark the 7 shapes on your grid and cut them out. Re-create the design shown here. Then invent your own new ones. Trace new designs, and challenge friends and family members to arrange the tangram pieces to match your designs.

BIRTHDAY GREETING POP-UP

Create a birthday greeting with a picture message that pops!

What You'll Need: Paper, scissors, ruler, markers or crayons, glue

Start by folding a piece of paper in half. Then cut 2 small parallel slits in the middle of the folded edge. Measure and mark the lines for the slits first, as shown, for easier cutting. Draw the lines about 1½ inches long, and about 1½ inches apart. Cut the slits, and push the square that is formed to the inside of the folded paper. Now, when the paper is opened up, the small square will stand up and out. This stand-up square becomes the mount for your pop-up piece. Cut out a heart, person, animal, or any other object or design to glue onto the square. You can use a drawing you've made yourself or one you've cut out of a magazine. After the pop-up piece is in place, color the background paper (adding scenery and other people and animals if you want) and include your birthday message. Your card is ready to bring a message with zing!

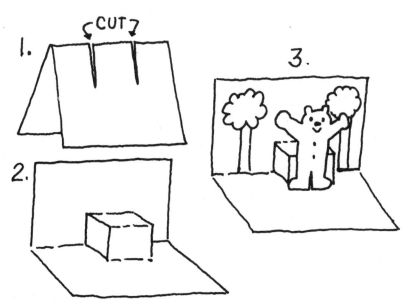

MAY DAY FLOWER CONE

54

Leave a lovely May Day flower surprise on someone's door as a springtime greeting!

What You'll Need: Decorated paper (see project 61), glue, hole punch, ribbon, paper towel, plastic bag, fresh flowers

Roll a piece of pretty paper into a cone shape, and glue the edges together to seal it. When the glue has dried, punch 2 holes on opposite sides of the cone. Tie the ends of a piece of ribbon through each of the holes to make a handle. Gather some fresh flowers. Put a wet paper towel around the flower stems and cover the towel with a plastic bag. Tie ribbon around the plastic bag to seal it, and set the flowers inside the decorative cone. Hang the cone on a family member's bedroom doorknob or on the front door of a neighborhood friend.

55

MAY DAY GARLAND

Celebrate the blossoming of the spring season with a floral crown!

What You'll Need: Fresh flowers, floral wire, scissors

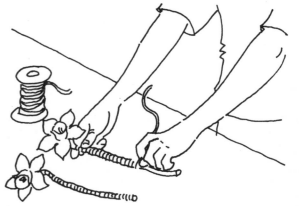

The arrival of spring is celebrated in many European countries on the first day of May. Flower garlands, crowns, and baskets full of flowers are part of many of the celebrations. To make a flower crown, gather 6 to 10 colorful flowers. Wrap green floral wire around the stem of each flower. Wind the wiry stem of each flower around the stem of the next flower, just beneath the flower. Weave the stem of the last flower around the stem of the first to form a circle. (Place the garland on your head to check the fitting before closing the circle.) Now don the floral crown, and celebrate spring!

CINCO DE MAYO FLOWERS

56

Make a festive floral bouquet to commemorate an important Mexican holiday.

What You'll Need: Different colors of tissue paper, scissors, chenille stems, ribbon

In Spanish, Cinco de Mayo means "the fifth of May." It was on this day in 1862 that a badly outnumbered Mexican army defeated the well-equipped invading French army. Now, May 5 is a holiday in Mexico. Celebrate this springtime holiday by making your own flowers. Cut tissue paper circles in a variety of colors in 3 different sizes. For each flower, use 2 small circles, 2 medium circles, and 2 large circles. Place 2 small circles on top of 2 medium circles, and put these on top of the 2 large circles. Make a U with the chenille stem, and push it through all 6 layers so that both ends of the chenille stem go all the way through the pile and stick out behind the large circles. Twist the chenille stem ends together on the bottom of the flower to make it into a stem. Fold up each circle to create a ruffle of petals. (You can make a flower using 1 color, 2 colors, or all different colors!) Make a few flowers, and put them in a vase or tie them together with a ribbon for festive holiday beauty.

MUD DECORATING

Paint with mud, as do the Korhogo people of the Ivory Coast in Africa.

What You'll Need: Mud, plastic bowl, pitcher, strainer, plastic spoon, water, paint, cotton cloth (old sheet, muslin, or handkerchief), paintbrush or leaf or twig, newspaper or brown grocery bag

To prepare your mud paint, dig up a cupful of dirt or mud. Gather together a plastic bowl, pitcher of water, strainer, and plastic spoon. Place a little of the dirt or mud in the strainer and add some water. Stir the mixture over the plastic bowl, removing pebbles, sticks, leaves, and other pieces that do not fit through the strainer. Continue to add and strain more mud, stopping occasionally to pour off the water that collects at top of the bowl as mud settles to the bottom. When the mud is fully strained and smooth, add some paint to the mud to create a rich, earthy color. Paint on cotton cloth as the Korhogo do: Place a handkerchief, piece of muslin, or cut section of an old sheet on newspaper, and paint the material with the mud using a paintbrush or a leaf or a twig. Or, paint on the newspaper or a grocery bag that's been cut open.

VIETNAMESE BEAN-BAG TOSS

*Grab a beanbag, and try your talent at **Da-Cau**, a game played by Vietnamese children.*

What You'll Need: Beanbag

The object of this game is to balance the game piece on your foot without letting it touch the ground, even when it's tossed! To play, place a beanbag on your foot, kick it up in the air, and then try and catch it by getting it to land back on the top of the same foot! If you are playing with a friend, toss the bag back and forth, foot to foot, without letting it land on the ground. To make the game more challenging, play it with a coin instead of a beanbag, just as Vietnamese children do!

LITTLE WORRIER DOLLS

Send your worries away by making miniature dolls who will do all your worrying for you!

What You'll Need: Aluminum foil, masking tape, newspaper, flour, water, bowl, plastic wrap, gesso (available at an art or craft store), paints, paintbrush

Follow this tradition of Central America and keep a set of dolls under your pillow. Each night before going to sleep, whisper a worry to each doll. After your troubles have been told, as the tradition goes, you can forget about them. The dolls will do all the worrying that's needed! To make the dolls, mold the basic body shape for each doll out of aluminum foil. You can mold the body all in 1 piece or create separate body parts and then attach them using masking tape. When the doll's shape is finished, cover the whole surface with masking tape. Now the dolls are ready for papier-mâché. Tear newspaper into small, thin strips and set aside. Mix a thick paste out of flour and water. Dip the newspaper strips into the paste, and lay them over the dolls. Cover each doll completely by overlapping the newspaper strips. Set the dolls on newspaper and let them dry for a day. Then cover them with a second coat of newspaper strips, and set them to dry again. (Keep the paste covered with plastic between uses.) When the dolls are fully dry, paint them with gesso. Let them dry again (15 minutes). Now paint the dolls in the colors of your choice. Let dry again, and then tell them your troubles!

HUICHOL INDIAN YARN PICTURE

60

Tell a story with a yarn picture as the Huichol Indians of western Mexico do.

What You'll Need: Pencil, cardboard, scissors, yarn, glue, craft stick

Brilliant Huichol pictures depict stories about the Indians' myths, religion, and history. To make your own colorful yarn picture, draw an outline of an animal, person, plant, or object on a piece of cardboard. Then cut and glue pieces of yarn on the outline to cover it—use the craft stick to apply the glue to the cardboard. Continue to add additional strands of yarn inside the outline, "painting" with yarn, until the design is filled up with color. Place yarn pieces close together so that only the yarn, and not the cardboard, shows. After the picture has been filled, you can use another color of yarn to fill up the space outside the animal, person, plant, or object your story is about.

61 # GIFT-WRAPPING PAPER

Make the gift wrapping as special as the gift!

What You'll Need: Food coloring or tempera paint, liquid starch, bowl, cardboard, scissors, newspaper, spoon, paper, sea sponge

For patterned gift wrap, mix food coloring or tempera paint with liquid starch in a bowl to make a thick paint. Make design combs by cutting cardboard into small rectangles 1 to 3 inches wide. Cut notches on one side of each rectangle, making variations in the rectangles so that each comb can be used to create a different effect. The notches can be cut closer or farther apart, the teeth can be wider or narrower, or you can even vary the width of the notches and teeth on a rectangle! Spread newspaper to cover the working surface. Lay your wrapping paper on the

newspaper, and, using the spoon, cover it with the finger paint. Use the notched edge of the cardboard squares to create designs in the paint by combing over the surface of the paper. For a textured wrapping paper, use the sea sponge to dab paint onto a piece of unpainted paper. Let the paper dry overnight.

SUMMERTIME WREATH

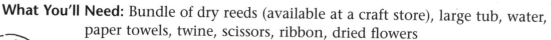

62

Follow a Swedish tradition—make a flower wreath to celebrate midsummer!

What You'll Need: Bundle of dry reeds (available at a craft store), large tub, water, paper towels, twine, scissors, ribbon, dried flowers

Place reeds in a large tub of warm water and soak them for 15 to 30 minutes to soften. Then dry the reeds with paper towels. Gently bend and mold the reeds to form a circle, overlapping the ends and tying them in place with twine. Also, tie the reeds together with twine at regular intervals (about 4 inches apart) all around the circle. Let the reeds dry completely. When the reeds are dry, insert the stems of dried flowers into the reeds, and secure them in place by tying pretty ribbons around the reeds and flower stems. To prepare your own dried flowers ahead of time, pick some wildflowers and tie them together with string. To dry, hang the bouquet upside down in a dark closet for several weeks.

OJO DE DIOS

63

Weave yarn around two sticks or twigs to create an ancient Mexican "Eye of God." It will watch over and protect you.

What You'll Need: 2 twigs or craft sticks, glue, yarn, scissors

To make your Ojo de Dios, glue 2 craft sticks to create an X shape. Or, if you use twigs, hold them in the X shape and tie them together by winding yarn around the cross section diagonally in 1 direction and then diagonally in the other direction. After you have formed the X, tie a strand of yarn to the center and begin to weave it around the arms of the X. Weave the yarn over and around 1 arm and then over and around the next arm. Continue in this way around the X. Change colors by tying a new piece of yarn to the end of the piece you have been using, and keep winding. Continue until the entire shape is covered, and then tuck the end of the yarn into the weaving. Add a dot of glue to hold the end in place.

64 LUNCH BAG KITE

Make your own paper bag kite as a way to join in the sky festivities that take place all around the globe!

What You'll Need: Yarn or string; scissors; yardstick; masking tape or stapler; lunch-size paper bag; crayons or markers; ribbon, wrapping paper, or tissue paper; glue; crepe paper streamer

Kites were invented 3,000 years ago in China, and they spread around the world from there. Today kites and kite festivals are a part of the traditions of many countries, including Guatemala, Japan, India, and Malaysia. Cut five 1-yard-long pieces of yarn or string. Tape or staple the end of each of 4 of the pieces to a corner of the open side of the bag. Tie the loose ends of the 4 pieces together. Tie the fifth piece (for holding the kite) to the end of the 4 knotted strings. Decorate the bag with crayons or markers and by gluing on ribbon, wrapping paper, or tissue paper. Attach a streamer to the bag's bottom, and run with it!

DREAM CATCHER 65

Make a Native American dream catcher to tangle up and trap bad dreams!

What You'll Need: Plastic coffee can lid, scissors, double-sided tape, ruler, hole punch, yarn, feather, beads and masking tape (optional)

To make the dream catcher, cut the center out of a plastic coffee can lid, leaving a 1-inch rim. Then cut 1-inch strips of double-sided tape, and tape them around the rim. Now punch a hole in the rim and tie a piece of yarn to the rim. Wind the yarn all the way around the rim to make a colorful covering. To change colors as you go, tie a different color of yarn to the end of the yarn you are winding. The double-sided tape will hold the yarn-covering in place. After the rim is covered with yarn, carefully pull apart the yarn in several places and punch additional holes around the rim. Loop a new piece of yarn through these holes, tie it to the rim, and then weave it through a hole across the rim, and keep repeating this procedure in a random pattern. Tie the end piece to the rim also. Tie 2 additional pieces of yarn onto the rim, 1 at the top to make a loop to hang the dream catcher, and 1 at the bottom with a feather tied to it. After the dream web is woven, push back the yarn rim covering to cover the web holes. To make the web more decorative, you can add beads to the yarn web as you weave it. (Wrap a piece of masking tape around the end of the yarn piece to make it easier to thread the beads onto the yarn.)

DAY OF THE DEAD COOKIES

Around the same time you celebrate Halloween, kids in Mexico are celebrating the Day of the Dead.

What You'll Need: ¼ cup margarine, ¼ cup butter, ⅓ cup sugar, 1 egg, ½ teaspoon vanilla, 1 cup flour, ½ teaspoon baking powder, ½ teaspoon salt, canned icing, mixing bowl, measuring cups and spoons, mixing spoon, rolling pin, dull knife, spatula, cookie sheet

In Mexico, the Day of the Dead is celebrated on November 2, All Souls' Day on the Christian calendar. On this day, Mexicans honor the dead with a celebration of life. Cookies and candies in the shape of skulls and skeletons are popular Day of the Dead treats. To make your own skull-shaped cookies, start by measuring and mixing together the margarine, butter, sugar, egg, and vanilla. When thoroughly blended, add the flour, baking powder, and salt. Chill dough in the refrigerator for an hour. After the dough is chilled, roll it out to approximately ⅛ inch thickness. Cut skull shapes out of the dough. Place cookies on an ungreased cookie sheet. Have an adult help you bake the cookies at 400 degrees for 6 to 8 minutes. When cookies are cool, decorate them using the icing. (Makes approximately 2 dozen cookies.)

TURKEY DAY DECORATION

Turn a ball of clay and a handful of cotton swabs into a fat turkey with a tailful of feathers.

What You'll Need: Modeling clay, stiff paper, scissors, crayons or markers, newspaper, paper cups, paint, cotton swabs

This clay turkey can be used as a colorful Thanksgiving decoration on a holiday dinner table, in a window, or even peeking out of a bookshelf. To make the turkey, roll some modeling clay into a ball for the turkey's body. Cut a turkey head and neck shape from a piece of stiff paper. Draw the turkey's eyes and color the head, beak, wattle, and neck. Insert the stiff paper head and neck piece into the clay body. Now you're ready for the tail! Lay newspaper on your work surface. Pour a small amount of several different colors of paint into different cups. Place the turkey and paint cups on the newspaper. Dip 1 side of the cotton swab in a paint cup, then insert the other end into the turkey's rump. Keep dipping and inserting until the turkey's tail is colorful and full.

ADVENT CALENDAR

Make your own Advent calendar, and count down the days to Christmas with your personalized pictures. Or make a countdown calendar to any special holiday or event!

What You'll Need: Tagboard, paper, craft knife, markers, tape, paper, scissors, pencil, gift box, yarn

To make a calendar, draw 24 small squares (for doors) on a piece of tagboard. Then get an adult to help you cut 3 sides of each door with the craft knife so that they can open and close. Tape paper to the back of the tagboard. Open each door and draw or paint a picture on the paper. Then close the door! Number the doors 1 to 24 in the order they are to be opened. Decorate the front of the calendar. For a fancier calendar, use a cardboard gift box. Cut the 24 doors out of the bottom of the box. Then cut out small ornaments (stars, birds, bells) from tagboard, and decorate them. Tape a piece of yarn to the back of each ornament. Tape the top piece of the yarn just above the door (on the inside of the box) so it can be seen hanging when the door is opened. Tape the box closed and set it on its side, number the doors, and decorate the front.

A SUNNY CALENDAR

The Gregorian calendar, which is the calendar used by most Western nations, is a solar calendar. A solar calendar charts time by the sun. Most other calendars are lunar calendars—they chart time by the moon. A solar year is actually 365 days, 5 hours, 48 minutes, and 46 seconds—which is why a day is added to February every 4 years!

YUT-NORI

69

This game has been popular in Korea for 1,000 years.

What You'll Need: Tagboard, 4 craft sticks, sticker dots, markers, game pieces

Korean children traditionally play this game between Lunar New Year and the first full moon. To make a board, cut out a square or circle from tagboard. Place the sticker dots in a border around the outside of the square or circle. Designate one dot as the starting place by using a different-colored or different-shaped sticker or by coloring around that dot with markers. Decorate the 4 craft sticks on 1 side only. To play the game, each player takes a turn tossing the sticks in the air. The player then moves a game piece according to how the sticks land. If all 4 sticks land with the decorated side up, the player moves 4 dots. If 3 sticks land with decorations up, the player moves 3 dots; 2 decorated sticks = 2 dots; 1 decorated stick = 1 dot. And if all the sticks land blank side up, the player moves 5 dots! If a player lands on a dot where another player's game piece is resting, the second player must go back to the starting dot. The first player all the way around the board is the winner.

70

SEED & BEAN NECKLACE

String a necklace of beans and seeds, and make nature jewelry as many people around the world do.

What You'll Need: Dried beans, seeds from fruits or vegetables, bowl, water, darning needle, thimble, paper towels, buttonhole thread or carpet thread

Gather together dried beans and seeds from fruits and vegetables (such as melons, squash, or corn). Wash the seeds, and soak the beans and seeds in water to soften them; some beans need to soak overnight. Then remove them from the water, and poke a hole in each using the needle and thimble. (Have an adult help you.) Spread the beans and seeds on a paper towel, and let them dry. Thread the needle with thread that is long enough to slip over your head for a necklace. String the seeds and beads in a pattern or design, and then tie the ends of the thread together.

FABULOUSLY FIT

Keeping fit is not only fun, it's important. You'll need your body for years and years to come. So why not do what you can to keep it healthy—starting now? Each of the creative activities in this chapter will not only stretch your imagination but your muscles as well. So get into the spirit! Start running, jumping, stretching, hopping, dancing, and lots more! You'll also get some exercises in just learning how your body works. So get fabulously fit, and you'll have loads of fun at the same time.

SNOW BOOT TWO-STEP

71

Track down this snowy game for frosty winter fun.

What You'll Need: Snow boots, winter clothes

When snowfall threatens your outdoor adventures, try this game on for size. This tough-to-master version of follow the leader requires 2 or more players. The leader makes a path in freshly fallen snow. His or her teammates must try to step in exactly the same spots. The object of the game is to make it seem as if only one person has taken a walk through the snow. Can you pull it off? It takes balance and agility! Be sure to bundle up to stay warm and dry.

LEAVE IT TO ME

When autumn leaves are falling, drop in on this sneaky game.

What You'll Need: Fall leaves, cardboard boxes

The object of this fast-paced game is to see how many leaves each player can collect without having them stolen by other players. Set boxes (one per player) about 15 feet apart in a leaf-covered park, yard, or playground. One player says "go," and the game begins. Grab handfuls of leaves and put them into your box. But watch carefully. You can steal leaves from other boxes to fill your own, so you'll want to guard your box as you go. Remember, your box can be robbed while you're out searching or stealing!

TURTLE TAILS

Don't pull your head in and hide. Make believe you're a turtle for a box full of fun.

What You'll Need: Green colored paper, masking tape, oversize cardboard boxes, tempera or watercolor paints, paintbrush

If you'd like, decorate the outside of the cardboard boxes to look like turtle shells. Make long strips of green paper to resemble turtle tails. Use tape to fasten the paper tail to your pants, and crawl inside the cardboard shell. As you wander around the room on all fours wearing your turtle goods, try to snag the other players' paper tails. The last turtle left with a paper tail of their own wins the game. But remember, no dropping your shell to make tail snagging easier, or you're out of the game.

HOP TO IT!

Test your sneakers to see if television advertisements are true.

What You'll Need: Dress shoes; sneakers; socks; chalk, tape, or washable marker

Ever wondered if the sport shoe commercials are true? Can different footwear help you jump farther? Better? Higher? This experiment can help you find out. Mark a starting point with chalk, tape, or washable marker on the sidewalk. Wearing your favorite sneakers, jump as far as you can from your starting point. Mark where you landed, and label it "sneakers." Now repeat the action in dress shoes, in socks, and in bare feet. How do the chalk marks compare?

STUFFY STACK

75

Build an adorable mountain with stuffed animals you love.

What You'll Need: Stuffed animals, measuring tape

Is your room overflowing with stuffed animals? See how your plush pals really stack up in this silly game. Carefully stack your puffy pets, measuring the pile each time you successfully add another beast. Write down your totals as you go to find out how high a stack you can make before it all falls down. Compete against a friend or against your own best score. Put your bigger stuffed animals on the bottom of the pile, and save the smallest for your mountain peak.

HIGHEST OF ALL

The Himalayas are the world's highest mountain range, containing all 10 of the world's highest peaks. In fact, the Himalayas include 14 peaks more than 8,000 meters high and some 200 peaks more than 6,000 meters high.

DRESS-UP RELAY

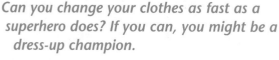

Can you change your clothes as fast as a superhero does? If you can, you might be a dress-up champion.

What You'll Need: Old clothes, at least 10 pieces for each team

The object of this game is to dress and undress as quickly as possible, regardless of where on your body the clothes actually wind up. Divide into 2 teams. Pile 10 clothing items for each team or player—anything from scarves to pants to shirts to purses to hats—at the opposite end of the room. When someone says "go," the first player on each team runs to the pile and puts on the clothes over his or her own, as quickly as possible. Anything goes, as long as nothing falls off your body as you run. The players run back to their starting point and take off the clothes. The next player on the team must put on the clothes, run back to the far side of the room, and take the clothes off. Then they sprint back to their team and touch the hand of the next player. The next player runs to the clothes and puts them on. The game goes on until the last player returns to the team. The first team to finish wins. You can even play this game on your own by racing against the clock. Keep trying to beat your best time!

BOOTING UP
Ever wonder why cowboys need boots? To keep their feet from slipping through their saddle stirrups, according to experts at the Cowboy Museum in Oklahoma.

WALK THE LINE

See if you can walk the walk the same way twice.

What You'll Need: 2 colors of chalk, colored yarn

Can you walk a straight line with your eyes open? Can you walk a straight line with your eyes closed? How about while you're holding your breath or singing a song? This will help you find out. Cover the bottom of your feet or shoes with dark-colored chalk. Now walk along a line of colorful yarn stretched across the sidewalk. Be sure you've used enough chalk on your shoes to leave a trail behind. Repeat the experiment with your eyes closed, using a different color of chalk. Compare the 2 trails. Remember that chalk can stain clothing, so wear old clothes when you experiment with this activity. And be sure to scrub your shoes or feet before you go into the house.

STRING ME ALONG

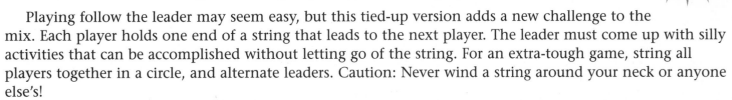

String your friends along for follow-the-leader fun!

What You'll Need: 2-foot lengths of string or yarn (one for each player)

Playing follow the leader may seem easy, but this tied-up version adds a new challenge to the mix. Each player holds one end of a string that leads to the next player. The leader must come up with silly activities that can be accomplished without letting go of the string. For an extra-tough game, string all players together in a circle, and alternate leaders. Caution: Never wind a string around your neck or anyone else's!

STRINGING YOU ALONG
Francis A. Johnson of Darwin, Minnesota, created the world's largest twine ball.
It's 12 feet wide and weighs 17,400 pounds.

SNOWSCAPE STOMP

79

Splashes of color make winter white a little warmer!

What You'll Need: Snow boots, tablespoon, paintbrushes, food coloring, paper cups, water

Does it look like winter weather has put a freeze on creative fun? Think again! Grab your gloves and your paintbrushes. That snowy hillside has just become an artist's canvas. Mix 2 tablespoons water with 10 drops food coloring in a paper cup (make as many colors as you desire). Go outside and march out a playful pattern of footprints in the snow. Splatter splashes of color in each frosty track, and watch the magic begin. Be sure to check for chilly changes later as the snow begins to melt and the colors soften. Remember that food coloring stains if it gets on clothing or light-colored boots, so be sure to wear old clothes your mom won't mind getting splattered. And don't forget to bundle up.

WHAT A FLAKE!

While it's true that no two are exactly alike, snowflakes can be broken down into six different six-sided crystal categories: needles, columns, plates, columns capped with plates, dendrites, and stars.

FEATHER FACE-OFF

Is soft still soft if you can't see what you're touching?

What You'll Need: Feathers, cloth, cotton balls, anything extremely soft to the touch, blindfold

Two players face each other, one blindfolded, one with a variety of soft objects in front of them. It's up to the blindfolded player to guess when the feather is being brushed across his or her cheek, rather than another very soft object. It's up to the sighted player to handle the objects so carefully that the blindfolded friend can't tell the difference. Remember, the gentler the pressure, the harder it is to tell what's touching you. Working on your senses (sense of touch) can be as fun as working on your muscles!

BALANCING ACT

Can you improve your balance? This game will help you find out.

What You'll Need: Book, stuffed animal, ball, paper cup

You may have seen people from other countries carrying jugs of water from village wells on their heads. How hard can it be? Find out by using different objects around the house. Set a book on your head, and keep track of how many steps you can take before the book topples. Do the same with a stuffed animal, a ball, and a paper cup. Compare your results. See if you can improve your balance by taking longer or shorter steps. Try moving your arms in different ways. Can you keep the objects on your head as you run or skip?

ALPHABET JUMP ROPE

82

Have some alphabet fun without skipping a beat.

What You'll Need: Jump ropes (one for each player)

cat

Pick a subject, such as animals, flowers, girls' names, or food. Then as you jump rope, name members of that group alphabetically (for the topic animals: ape, bear, cat, dog, elephant, fish) every other hop. If you miss while jumping or can't come up with the next animal or item in the alphabetical list, start over at the beginning. This game is great alone, but it's also fun to do with a friend.

83

SQUARE-A-ROUND

Square up with this ball tossing fun!

What You'll Need: 15×15-inch cloth squares or bandannas, fabric paint, paintbrush, tennis balls

First, using fabric paints you can buy at a craft or hobby store, decorate your square of fabric or bandanna to reflect your own personal style. If you love astronomy, you might decorate it with stars and planets. If you love dinosaurs, draw a Tyrannosaurus rex on your cloth. Once the paint dries, use the cloth to toss and catch tennis balls. How many tosses can you catch in a row without dropping your ball? How high can you make your toss? How many balls can you toss and catch in 1 minute? The possibilities are endless. For an extra challenge, play this game with a partner, tossing a single ball from cloth to cloth or making 2 balls cross in midair.

BOOT HILL

84

Slip out of your shoes and into some fun!

What You'll Need: Players' shoes, whistle

All players remove their shoes and put them in a pile at the center of the room. Mix the pile completely. The players form a circle around the pile, with everyone standing about 10 feet away from it. When the whistle sounds, the players head for the pile. The first player to find both of his or her own shoes and puts them on wins.

85

JUMPING JACK FLASH

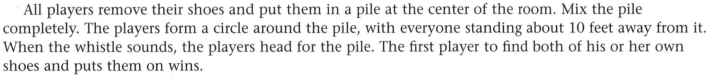

Want to build your biceps? Pump your pecs? Give your heart some heft? Check out this jumping jack flash.

What You'll Need: Paper, markers

Start your exercise routine with 5 jumping jacks on your first fitness day. Mark it on your fitness chart. Add 5 more the second day. Mark that on your chart. Keep adding 5 until you can do 25 jumping jacks with ease. Now, add a second exercise (like toe touches) to your routine, starting with 5 repetitions. Mark that exercise on your chart. Keep increasing repetitions and adding exercises. Before you know it, you'll be buff as can be.

ALL EARS!
Balance is all in your head—or rather your inner ear. The eighth cranial nerve (the vestibulocochlear nerve), which is deep inside your ear, translates sound waves and then carries nerve impulses for balance from the ear to the brain.

DRUMMER'S MARCH

86

Bang the gong, all day long.

What You'll Need: Round oatmeal boxes, scissors, tape, ribbon or string, construction paper, colorful markers, spoons

Make a drum from an oatmeal box. Be sure to decorate your drum to make it your own. Now dangle the drum from your neck using ribbon or string taped to the sides. Grab a couple of spoons (wooden or serving) to use as drumsticks, and you're on your way. Try singing your own songs or drumming along to music you hear on TV or the radio.

SHOESTRING TIE-UP

87

You'll have your hands full with these shoes!

What You'll Need: Old sneakers with long shoelaces, a stopwatch

Your shoe won't have to fit your foot for this fun race against the clock. The trick is in tying the shoe as you hold it in your hands. And did we mention, when you can't see it? How fast can you tie a shoe? How fast can you tie a shoe behind your back? This silly game will test your skills. Race against your own best time or compete against a friend. Place untied shoes at one end of the room, players at the other. Say "go," and have the runners race to the shoes and tie them. Time each player with a stopwatch. Now untie the shoes and repeat the process, but this time, tie the shoes while holding them behind your back. The player with the best scores wins.

SNEAKER FACT
The first sneaker widely sold in North America was the Converse All Star basketball sneaker, and it debuted in 1917.

BASKETBALL BUDDIES

88

You could sink this one with a smile!

What You'll Need: Basketball, chalk

Love shooting hoops? Why not add a few extra "grins" to the game? Each time you sink a basket, draw a facial feature on your ball. It could be an eye, a mouth, ears, even long, lush lashes. You're the winner—it's up to you to decide! Want to turn this activity into a competition? Decide on 5 facial features in advance. Each of you label a side of the basketball for your face. The first person to sink 5 baskets (and complete the facial expression) wins the game!

89

MILK BOTTLE WORKOUT

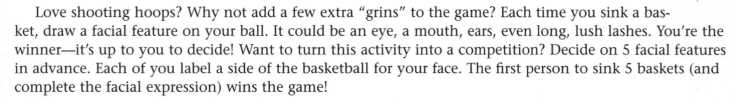

Milk this activity for all the fitness you can!

What You'll Need: Clean, used 1-quart plastic milk bottles; pebbles

Fill two 1-quart plastic milk bottles with pebbles. How many times can you lift those milk bottles, one in each hand, over your head before your arms get tired? How many times can you touch the bottles together behind your back? In front of you? How many times can you touch your toes with the bottles? Try this game once a week and see if your numbers improve.

HEART HEALTHY FUN
Aerobic exercises help keep your most important muscle strong—your heart.

HOP (AND POP) SCOTCH

90

Hop up for a surprising new twist on an old game.

What You'll Need: Chalk, small balloons, bean bags

Hopscotch just got explosive, thanks to this new idea. Rather than hopping on one foot, hold a small air-filled balloon between your feet as you hop. How long will your balloon last? Only time will tell. No matter how long you keep your balloon from bursting, no matter how good you get, there's always room to compete with yourself. For an extra challenge, hopscotch backward. Set up your hopscotch course on grass using thick, oversize color chalk to make the game a little safer. (Always remember to pick up balloon pieces, which are dangerous for small children and animals!)

91

BUNNY HOP

Egg-ceptional fun for somebunny smart!

What You'll Need: Paper plate, markers, cardboard boxes, plastic Easter eggs

Decorate a paper plate with your favorite spring or Easter designs. Put a cardboard box at one end of the room and another box filled with plastic Easter eggs at the other. Keep your feet together to make hopping the only way to go. Fill your paper plate with eggs, and carefully make your way to the box. Deliver your load, then hop back for more. Time yourself to see how quickly you can get the job done. Then try the game again to improve on your personal best. More than 1 person raring to play? Divide into teams for competitive fun.

HAPPENING JOINTS

92

Celebrate the bends and bounces of your body!

Every joint in your body is a kind of engineering wonder, designed to make your body move in amazing ways. So why not celebrate every single bend? Move from the tips of your fingers to the tips of your toes, flexing each joint. Count how many joints you can move independently. Imagine what it would be like if that particular joint didn't exist.

93

SHOE BOX SHUFFLE

See if these funny shoes box you in.

What You'll Need: 2 shoe boxes, paints or markers, yarn, scissors

You wear shoes everyday. But what happens when you strap on the boxes that came with the shoes? You wind up with some silly, slippery action you won't want to miss. Decorate your cardboard shoe boxes with paint and markers. Don't decorate the bottom of your shoe boxes—it's beauty you'll never see, and it might rub off on floors and carpets. Tie the boxes to your feet with yarn shoelaces, then take a walk, march, or wander. See how lucky you are to have feet a good deal smaller than these clunky "shoes."

GOOD MEDICINE
What are devil's shoestrings? Not flaming laces! It's a plant used for medicines that stop painful cramps.

SNOW SNAKES

94

Create wondrous winter snakes that won't hibernate!

What You'll Need: Snowy field, warm clothes and gloves, bits of food

Everyone's heard of a snowman. But making a slithering snow snake is ssssserious fun. Instead of making a snowman of 3 large balls, try a snow snake made of as many basketball-size snow sections as you can make. Once you've lined your snow snake balls up, carve out a pointed head and rattling tail at either end of the snake. Decorate your snake with bits of food, such as raisins. These will be good treats for hungry birds and squirrels.

95

HIKE AND HUNT

Keep your eye on the great outdoors!

What You'll Need: Plastic magnifying glass, paper, pencil

The next time you take a hike in the woods or a nature area in your neighborhood, keep your eyes open for signs of wildlife. Are there bird feathers on the trail? Have local animals left tracks in the mud or sand? Are there bits of fur trapped in the bushes? What signs of nature can you find? What clues do those signs offer to the animals' ways of life? Use the magnifying glass for up-close looks at items that catch your eye. Make notes of your observations. Then, hike the same path a week later and make more observations. What has changed? What hasn't? You can hike and observe regularly over a longer period and keep a nature journal. So learn something while you are exercising those legs!

FRANTIC FLYING DISK

96

Free your flying disk to sail to new heights!

What You'll Need: Flying disk (such as a Frisbee), hula hoop

Tossing a flying disk with a friend or a dog is a great way to keep fit—and it's fun to do all by yourself also! And you can add a new challenge to the popular game. See how easy (or how hard) it is to send your flying disk sailing through a hula hoop from 5 paces away. Too easy? Move back 10 paces from the hoop. Still not tough enough? Try it from 16 paces away. This game makes a great competition between friends or whole teams.

97

CHALK TALK HOP

Chalk it up to your winning ability to rhyme!

What You'll Need: Sidewalk chalk, knee pads

Take action with words in this colorful rhyming/jumping game. Draw five 2-foot squares in different colors on a cement or blacktop surface (such as a driveway, a sidewalk, or a playground). The squares should touch each other. Now hop from one square to the next. If you hop on the pink square, stop and write a word that rhymes with pink (such as "ink") in the box before you move on. Hopping on blue? Write a word such as "true." Get the picture? Can't think of a word that rhymes? You'll have to skip that box and leap to the next one. Any direction, forward, backward, or sideways is fair. A round is complete as soon as you rhyme every square. Be careful of your knees when jumping across pavement. Knee pads will come in handy for this game.

FAST CLAP

98

How fast can you clap your hands? It's not as easy as you think.

What You'll Need: Paper, pen or pencil, stopwatch or clock

We often clap our hands together to express our approval—to say we loved a musical show, to praise our favorite football players, to say we agree with something we've just heard. But how fast can you clap your hands? And how do those numbers change with the position of your arms? Write down your numbers to find out. Clap your hands in the usual position, right in front of your body, for 30 seconds. How many claps did you manage to make? Now do the same with your hands over your head. Now do the same with your hands behind your back. What muscles did you use when you clapped over your head that you didn't use clapping in front of you or clapping behind your back?

99

TEN-PENNY PICKUP

Once you toss these pennies, the race is on!

What You'll Need: 10 pennies, small box or bowl, paper, pencil or pen, stopwatch or clock

Hold 10 pennies in your hand, and softly scatter them just a few feet in front of you. See how fast you can gather the pennies and drop them in the box or bowl. Write down your time. Now repeat the process. But this time, gather them with your toes before dropping them in the bowl or box. How long did that take? Want a few more choices? Try picking up the pennies with only your right hand. Now, only your left hand. For extra fun, invite a friend to play with you, and see who's the penny pickup champion. Don't forget to wash your hands after you have finished playing. Coins are valuable, but they are not very clean!

LOSING YOUR MARBLES

100

Can you shoot your marbles straight enough to win this game?

What You'll Need: About 10 marbles, a carpeted room, a clock

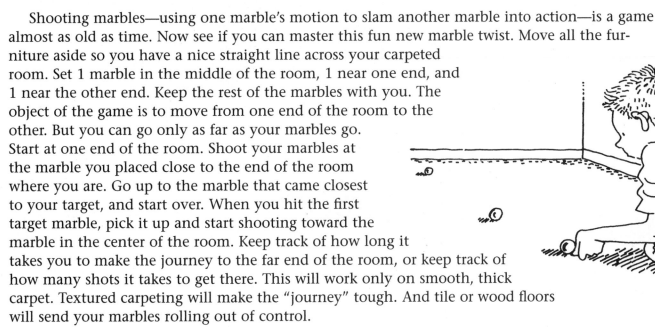

Shooting marbles—using one marble's motion to slam another marble into action—is a game almost as old as time. Now see if you can master this fun new marble twist. Move all the furniture aside so you have a nice straight line across your carpeted room. Set 1 marble in the middle of the room, 1 near one end, and 1 near the other end. Keep the rest of the marbles with you. The object of the game is to move from one end of the room to the other. But you can go only as far as your marbles go. Start at one end of the room. Shoot your marbles at the marble you placed close to the end of the room where you are. Go up to the marble that came closest to your target, and start over. When you hit the first target marble, pick it up and start shooting toward the marble in the center of the room. Keep track of how long it takes you to make the journey to the far end of the room, or keep track of how many shots it takes to get there. This will work only on smooth, thick carpet. Textured carpeting will make the "journey" tough. And tile or wood floors will send your marbles rolling out of control.

STEP BY STEP

101

Count on this step-by-step activity to be fun!

How many steps does it take to get from your room to your front door? How many steps to walk to school? How many steps to explore your local mall? You've never thought about it, right? Well, slip on your thinking cap, and take it step by step. You might be amazed at how busy your feet actually are. Want an extra mind bender? Get an adult in your house to count his or her steps on the same routes you selected, then compare the numbers. Why are they different?

FEATHER FLOAT

102

Can you keep your fluffy feather afloat?

What You'll Need: Small feather

As light as a feather—we've all heard it said. But how light are feathers? And how easy to keep afloat? Lightly toss your downy feather in the air. Now try to position yourself exactly beneath the feather. Use your own personal air power to blow upward and keep the feather in the air. Note how long you can keep it from touching the ground. For extra fun, play the game with a friend.

103

DANCE PARTY

Dance to your own drummer, and see if you've got what it takes.

What You'll Need: Radio

Music video dancers, dancers on Broadway in New York, ballet dancers, dancers of all kinds are incredible athletes. If you don't believe it, try this simple exercise on for size. Wait for your favorite song to come on the radio. Begin to dance nonstop to the beat of the tune. Lift your legs, swing your arms, leap and twirl in the air. It doesn't really matter what you do, so long as you keep your body in constant motion for the entire length of the song. When the song ends, how does your body feel? How are your lungs feeling? Is your heart pumping at a rapid pace? Why do you think that's so? Now imagine dancing like that in a 50-minute ballet. You'll have a newfound respect for the professional dancers you love to watch on TV!

TUNE IN!
Did you know August 20 is National Radio Day? Why not tune in to celebrate all those disc jockeys you listen to!

TIP TO TIP

104

Try walking in a straight line as you've never done it before.

What You'll Need: Ruler

Have you ever seen an adult measure out the length or width of a room or space by walking very carefully, touching the heel of one shoe against the toe tip of the other? Try walking some of your favorite routes using that strange measuring method for steps. Does it take longer to accomplish the task? Is it harder to get from here to there? How many steps did you count to move from place to place? How did it make your legs feel? Measure a few of your favorite outdoor paths. Just for fun, measure your foot with a ruler to see exactly how long your favorite walks might be.

105

SQUIRT BOTTLE TAG

Here's a wet wonder to heat up (and cool down) your summer.

What You'll Need: Clean, empty dishwashing liquid bottles; water; tissues; masking tape

This fun tissue tag is a great way to beat the summer heat. Slip into your favorite swimming suit. Then tape an ordinary tissue to each player's back. The object of the game is to flood your fellow players' tissues with enough water to cause them to tear from the masking tape and fall to the ground. The last player with a tissue still in place wins the game.

ROLLING RIOT

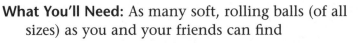

"The more the merrier" applies when it comes to this rolling riot.

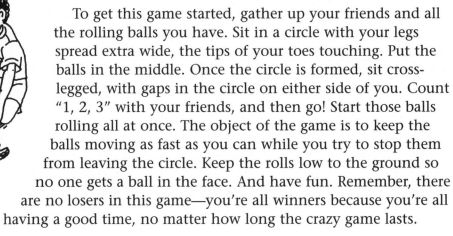

What You'll Need: As many soft, rolling balls (of all sizes) as you and your friends can find

To get this game started, gather up your friends and all the rolling balls you have. Sit in a circle with your legs spread extra wide, the tips of your toes touching. Put the balls in the middle. Once the circle is formed, sit cross-legged, with gaps in the circle on either side of you. Count "1, 2, 3" with your friends, and then go! Start those balls rolling all at once. The object of the game is to keep the balls moving as fast as you can while you try to stop them from leaving the circle. Keep the rolls low to the ground so no one gets a ball in the face. And have fun. Remember, there are no losers in this game—you're all winners because you're all having a good time, no matter how long the crazy game lasts.

BALL FOR ALL

Have a ball finding out how different "different" can be.

What You'll Need: Variety of balls (kick ball, football, baseball, basketball, Ping-Pong ball, golf ball, tennis ball, etc.)

Playing ball is pretty easy. But how simple is it really? Does one ball kick like another? Can you throw one ball as far as the next? Select 4 different balls (of 4 different shapes and sizes). Toss each ball as hard as you can. How far does the first ball go? How far does the second ball go? Now try to bounce each ball. How hard (or how easy) is that task? This fun experiment will help you find out how complicated playing ball can be.

SPIN AND TOUCH

108

How does balance affect the simple things you do?

Our balance depends on the workings of our inner ear. And spinning around in circles certainly affects our sense of balance. But how does being dizzy affect the little things we do? To find out, spin around in place 10 times or so. (Be sure you are somewhere that you won't hurt yourself if you fall!) Now see if you can touch your nose on the first try. See if you can easily walk a straight line. See if you can stand on one foot without a sway or tilt.

109

AFTERNOON MARATHON

Race through your afternoon routine, just for fun!

If getting your homework done after school isn't easy for you, turn it into a race against yourself. Grab a healthy snack when you first get home. As you nibble, go over your assignments, your after-school game plan. You'll grab your pencil, you'll open your science book, you'll read your chapter, you'll answer the true and false questions, you'll slurp a drink of water, you'll tackle your spelling words with a smile. The minute your snack is gone, make a note of the time and spring into action. Speed through your homework to see how fast you can put it behind you. Try to carve a little off your time every day. But be careful to do your homework correctly, not just fast! And be careful not to gobble your snack too quickly either.

FROM WHERE TO WHERE?

The modern marathon commemorates the run of Pheidippides, in 490 B.C., from Marathon, Greece, to Athens. He was running to tell of Greece's victory over the Persians. Legend has it that Pheidippides ran into Athens, delivered his message, "Nike!" (Victory!), and then died.

PAPER PLANE LIFT-OFF

110

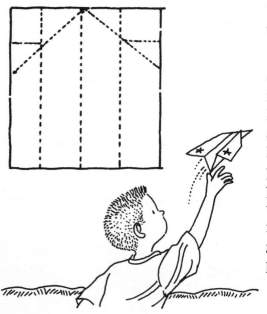

How your plane flies depends a lot on you!

What You'll Need: Paper, crayons or markers, chalk

Fold your favorite airplane out of a crisp, clean piece of paper. Decorate it with crayons or markers. Now launch your flying machine at your favorite playground, and mark where it lands with a piece of chalk. Try tossing it with your other hand, and mark where it lands. Toss it twice as hard, and mark where it lands. Try it with half the force you originally used. Has the wind picked up? Has it gone still? See how that affects your flights. Will your paper plane fly straight up? Will it crash if you launch it toward the ground? Who knows? But give it a try, and be sure to mark where the flights land. Then compare your marks on the ground, and try to figure out just what it would take to launch the perfect flight.

111

CAT WALKING

This purrrfectly wonderful activity will keep you on your toes.

Scientists say cats actually walk on their toes at least 80 percent of the time. Could you manage that? Practice walking on your toes to your favorite song, counting 1, 2, 3, 4, 5, 6, 7, 8 as you go. When you get to 9 and 10, walk as you normally do. Start your cat walk again, counting 1, 2, 3, 4, 5, 6, 7, 8, then walking flat-footed again for steps 9 and 10. How do your legs feel? Want to test a new catlike rhythm? Do the same cat walk to the beats of your name.

HELPING HANDS

Everyone—kids, grown-ups, plants, and animals alike—needs help every now and then. This section gives you the chance to lend your very special assistance. Thanks to these activities, you'll soon discover the proud, warm feeling that comes from giving of yourself. And in the process, you'll let someone know that you care! (Be sure to get your parents' permission before doing any of these projects.)

CRAFT STICK STICK-INS

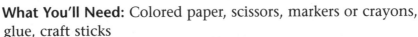

112

Dress up hospital plant life with colorful craft-stick fun.

What You'll Need: Colored paper, scissors, markers or crayons, glue, craft sticks

Many hospital patients and senior citizens get plants as gifts. These adorable stick-ins can spruce up those plants to make a real cheer-up treat. On colored paper, draw and cut out a butterfly, a ladybug, a bird, or any other design you like. Decorate your designs so they are really special. Glue your paper design to the end of a craft stick (or a clean ice cream stick). Use the other end of the stick to anchor the paper design in the potting soil. Share these cheerful stick-ins with people who might not be able to get out and enjoy the great outdoors.

POST OFFICE

Say you care, even if you don't know the person you're saying it to.

What You'll Need: Paper, pens or markers, tape

Everyone loves getting mail—especially soldiers far from home or senior citizens without families of their own. You can help cheer up these sometimes forgotten citizens by writing short, encouraging notes all your own. Remind the folks you write to that people care about them. Tell them to have a great day. Fold the letter into a rectangle and seal it with a piece of tape. Address it to "You" from "Me," but don't include your real name or address. Take your letters to your local senior citizens home or Red Cross office. They'll do the rest.

DOT ART

114

Here's a whole new angle on dot-to-dot pictures!

What You'll Need: White paper, markers, colored paper, hole punch, glue

Want a new art project sure to cheer up a neighbor and maybe make you a new friend? Try dot art. Draw a picture on a plain sheet of white paper. Punch tiny round dots from sheets of colored paper, using a hole punch. When you punch, hold the colored paper over a different sheet of white paper to catch the dots as they fall. Glue the colorful dots in place on your drawing, leaving as little white as possible without letting the dots overlap. Your finished work will have a bright, unusual look. Share these drawings with lonely neighbors who could use a lift.

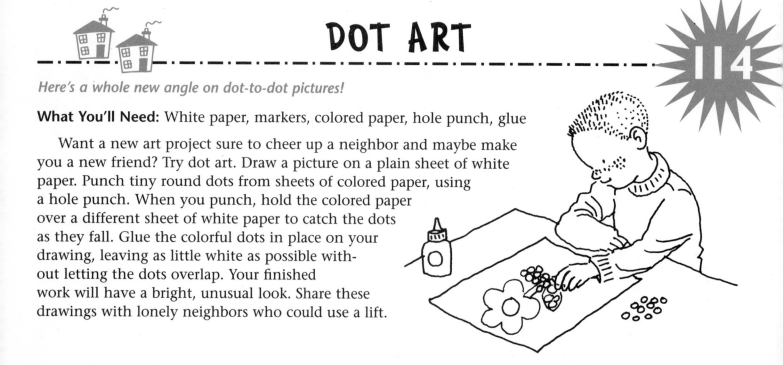

PENCIL PALS

Coil up with a new friend!

What You'll Need: Self-hardening (air-drying) clay, white glue, wiggle eyes, markers, pencils, wire rack

Kids with learning disabilities sometimes need a special friend to help them stay focused and eager to learn. These cute pencil pals might be just what the teacher ordered. Roll the clay into 3-inch "snakes" that are ¼ inch wide. Glue 2 wiggle eyes to the head end of the snake, and draw on a silly smile. Coil the snake around the eraser end of a number 2 pencil. Use markers to decorate the snake's skin with fun patterns and colors. Make a few different snakes. Lay the pencils on the wire rack, and allow 2 days for the clay to harden. Add a little white glue around the snake to guarantee that it will stay put. Donate these pencil pals to your school's special education or resource room teachers.

KIDS LIKE YOU

Disabled students seem to have one wish in common, no matter what their physical or mental challenge. "Just treat them like normal kids," say special education experts, "and try to understand they have feelings, too."

POP CAN CUT-UPS

Save an animal's life with scissors and glue.

What You'll Need: Blank paper, colored markers or crayons, masking tape, stapler

Every year, thousands of birds, sea creatures, and forest animals lose their lives after becoming entangled in plastic pop-can caddies—those plastic binders that keep aluminum six-packs together until shoppers get them safely home. You can help save animals' lives by spreading the word. Make simple flyers that ask your neighbors to be pop can cut-ups: Ask them to snip those dangerous bits of plastic into harmless strips. Pass your flyers out to your neighbors. Be sure to ask for permission before you post them in public places, such as malls or schools. And always take a trusted adult with you.

CHALK IT UP TO PATRIOTISM

Make your voice heard—even before you can vote!

What You'll Need: Colored chalk

People under 18 can't vote to make legal changes in the United States, but they can remind neighborhood adults to exercise their civic duty. When election day rolls around in your neighborhood . . . take to the sidewalks. Use colored chalk to write this one powerful word on the cement squares all around your neighborhood: VOTE! Then you will have done your part without taking sides. Remember to ask permission before writing on the sidewalk in front of someone's house.

"LEAVE" A TREAT

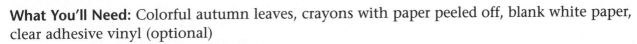

118

Bring a little autumn beauty to someone who needs it.

What You'll Need: Colorful autumn leaves, crayons with paper peeled off, blank white paper, clear adhesive vinyl (optional)

Busy grown-ups sometimes forget to stop and watch the leaves change color when autumn rolls around. You can remind your favorite adult how beautiful the seasons can be. Gather flat, flexible autumn leaves that have just fallen from their branches. Select colors of crayons similar to the colors of the leaves. One by one, slip the leaves under a blank piece of paper, and gently rub the side of a crayon back and forth across the surface of the paper over the leaf. An image of the leaf will appear. Repeat the process with other leaves of various shapes and colors until your page is a colorful fall collage. Share it with a busy friend. If you'd like, cover your collage with clear adhesive vinyl for a placemat or more permanent art.

SPOON UP SOME FUN

119

A spoonful of fun makes these puppets a real treat!

What You'll Need: Clean plastic spoons, small poms, colored paper, scissors, glue, wiggle eyes, small paper cups

Sick kids deserve a lift. So spoon up some fun with these wacky spoon puppets! Glue poms and colored paper to the bowl of a plastic spoon to create a colorful face. Add wiggle eyes. Cut out paper bunny, puppy, clown, or other ears, and glue them on. Pass these plastic pals out to kids ages 5 and up in your local children's hospital. Stay a while to help put on shows, if the hospital will let you. Make a miniature puppet theater by cutting a slit in the bottom of a small paper cup. Stick the spoon end down through the cup opening and through the slit. Use the spoon handle to push the puppet out of the cup and perform the show!

CRICKET KIT

This chirping chum is a good-luck friend everyone can enjoy.

120

What You'll Need: Clear plastic jar, nail, cotton ball, cat food, cricket

Most kids love keeping pets. But some apartment landlords won't allow the privilege. If you have a friend who really wants to care for a critter, this cricket kit could be the perfect gift. Keeping crickets is fun and easy. Search your yard for a cricket. If it's winter or extremely cold outside, you might have to turn to your local pet store to buy a cricket (for about a dime). Wash the jar thoroughly. Have an adult help you poke a few air holes in the upper edge of a clean plastic jar (such as an empty peanut butter jar) with the nail. Slip your cricket into the jar along with a cotton ball soaked with water and a little cat food crushed to a fine powder. Give the jar to your friend and watch him or her grin. Remind your friend to feed and water the cricket every other day. Give your friend a few extra cotton balls for water and a plastic bag full of crushed cat chow, just to get them started. And tell them the crickets should live at least 3 months (sometimes longer).

ANIMAL DREAMS
What do homeless kids miss most? According to one recent survey, household pets.

PENNIES FOR PETS

Raising money for animal shelters is easy if you do it a penny at a time.

What You'll Need: Empty coffee cans with lids, colored paper, tape, colorful markers or crayons

Community animal shelters take in lost or abandoned pets and search for new homes for the creatures. Most get their money from the American Humane Society, the Dumb Friends League, your city government, or other special agencies. But no matter who pays the bills, there never seems to be enough money to go around. You can help by collecting pennies. Cover an empty coffee can with colored paper. Then decorate the paper with pet drawings, and label it "Pennies for Pets." Once a week, ask your mother, your father, your grandmother, even your aunt, if they have any extra pennies they can spare. Or do chores to earn a few coins. Explain that you are collecting pennies for your local animal shelter. Once your can is full, count the pennies and present them to the shelter director. You'll feel good, and you'll be an animal-loving hero.

BOOKMARKS THE SPOT

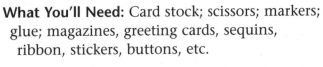

Make someone's leisure reading even more fun.

What You'll Need: Card stock; scissors; markers; glue; magazines, greeting cards, sequins, ribbon, stickers, buttons, etc.

People who can't get around much, such as the elderly or sick, often find reading to be a cheerful escape. You can add an extra spark of warmth to their reading by making colorful bookmarks. Cut 2×5-inch strips of card stock. Decorate the strips with colorful designs or inspirational sayings cut out from magazines or greeting cards and lots of bright bits and pieces you find around the house. Ask your local senior center or home for the elderly to pass them out to folks who might need a little lift—or ask permission to go to the center and hand them out yourself. The personal touch may really touch some seniors' lives!

STAR POWER

123

Create a little sparkle power for your youngest friends.

What You'll Need: Poster board, scissors, aluminum foil, glitter glue (optional), string, 3 drinking straws

The next time your baby brother or sister is hit with teething pain, the flu, or a sniffling cold, you can be the baby's favorite star. Cut out 8 poster-board stars of different sizes. Cover both sides with aluminum foil. Use the glitter glue to decorate them if you'd like. Carefully poke a hole in a tip of each star. Slip a piece of string through each hole. Using string, tie 2 of the drinking straws to the ends of the other. Dangle the sparkling stars from drinking straws and suspend the finished mobile (out of reach) from a toddler's ceiling or door frame. It's sure to cheer up even a cranky little friend.

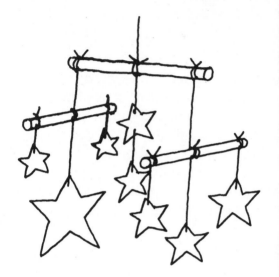

NEW KID COMRADE

124

Being new to a school is always hard. You can lighten the load for a new kid in your class.

Moving to a new town and a new school is never easy. But you can help. The next time a new student enrolls in your class, volunteer to show them around the school. Introduce them to all your friends. Sit with them at lunch. Invite them to play with your friends at recess. Ask a few friendly questions: "Where did you live before you moved? Do you have any brothers or sisters? Do you have any pets? What's your favorite after-school hobby?" All this will make a very difficult day a little easier for a nervous new student. And you might make a new friend along the way!

125

EDIBLE NECKLACES

Jewelry you can eat makes a super gift for yourself or others.

What You'll Need: Spoon, plastic sandwich bags, colorful and fun cereals, dried fruits, healthy candy snacks, curling ribbon

Special snacks are hard to afford when you live from moment to moment in a homeless shelter. So give a needy kid a treat by making and sharing these delicious edible necklaces. Wash your hands carefully. Spoon the cereal and other snacks into a plastic sandwich bag. Use the curling ribbon to tie off the bag. Leave the ends of the ribbon long so you can curl them so they look pretty. Make a long necklace out of more curling ribbon, and tie it to the bag so the bag looks like a large charm—be sure the necklace is long enough to slip over someone's head. Call your local YMCA or social services hotline for suggestions on where to donate your snacks.

SHOW THEM YOU CARE
Sadly, children are one of the fastest growing groups of poor people in America. Helping homeless children will let them know that someone really cares.

VACATION BACK-UP

126

When your neighbors go on vacation, offer to lend a hand.

When your neighbors find the time to visit distant relatives, the Grand Canyon, or the museum of their dreams, you can help make their trip carefree. Volunteer to gather their mail each day and keep it until they get home. Offer to water their prize roses or even feed their pet fish while they're gone. You'll be a hero in their book! They might even send you a postcard while they're away. But be careful: Don't let anyone know your neighbors are gone, not even your very best friend. It's important that this remain a confidential good deed, just to protect your neighbors' privacy.

127

CHEF'S DELIGHT

Be a "hamburger helper," and make your favorite grown-up very happy.

If your parents or caretakers have had one of those busy days, why not volunteer to make life a little easier at dinner time? Stand ready in the kitchen to fetch every spice or ingredient the cook might need. Set the table, and gather the dirty dishes without being asked. Offer to load the dishwasher or scrub the dirty dishes while your favorite grown-up takes a moment to relax. You're bound to be the chef's delight when you lend a helping hand.

TV TALK

128

Save a senior some time—offer a few TV tips!

What You'll Need: Paper, pen, newspaper TV program listing

What does your favorite senior citizen watch on TV? Nature programs? Musical specials? Classic movies? Ask him or her. Then go through your local television guide and copy information about the programs you think they would most enjoy in large, easy-to-read print. For regular weekly programs, you can make a personal guide once a month. Update it for specials once a week. If you don't know a senior citizen, ask your local elderly living center if there is a "grandparent" you can adopt for this project.

129

STAINED GLASS

Create beautiful stained glass—without the glass.

What You'll Need: Colored, nonbleeding tissue paper; glue; clear acrylic sheet; paintbrush

Using pieces of brightly colored tissue paper, glue, and a sheet of clear acrylic, create "stained glass" decorations to share with shut-ins. These window ornaments are especially nice during the dreary winter months. Use a paintbrush to spread glue on the clear acrylic. Glue tissue paper in patterns to the acrylic sheet, being sure to cover all open areas. Once the design is completely dry, your design will lift off the acrylic sheet. Moisten a window lightly with water, and press your "glass" into place. The light shining through the "stained glass" will be beautiful!

TELEPHONE SMILES

130

Send a smile from phone to phone.

What You'll Need: Telephone, yellow pages

Sometimes, just a friendly hello can inspire a warm grin. With your telephone in hand, you can spread smiles without ever leaving home. Contact your local nursing home. Ask them if any of the residents could use a friendly call. Then spread the news—someone cares and isn't afraid to say so. Before you call a resident, think of some topics of conversation so you'll be sure to have something to talk about. Be sure to ask about them as people—older people have lived long lives, and they have some fascinating stories to tell! Some ideas to talk about are where the senior grew up and went to school, what their favorite TV shows are, what they like to read, etc. An adult might be able to help you brainstorm more ideas.

131

BACKYARD BINGO

Become a bingo winner and recycle at the same time.

What You'll Need: Trash bags, work gloves

Want to put an environmental spin on an old favorite? Play Backyard Bingo. Gather a team of friends and neighbors together for a clean-up day. Grab some trash bags and put on your work gloves, then search your yard or neighborhood park for bits of trash with the letters "b," "i," "n," "g," and "o" printed on them. The first person to collect all 5 letters—and securely dispose of the garbage—wins the game. But in the long run everyone wins, because a cleaner park is a safer park. Be extra careful of broken glass. Ask for adult assistance to clean up dangerous shattered glass or any other items you're unsure of.

IN A NUTSHELL

132

These are tiny bird feeders you can give to friends.

What You'll Need: Nutshells, peanut butter, birdseed, ribbon, nontoxic glue

The next time you feel like a nut, save the shell. Your local seniors will thank you. Fill an empty nutshell with smooth peanut butter. Sprinkle the peanut butter with birdseed. Glue ribbon on the shells to attach the tasty treats to the branches of trees near the windows of a nearby nursing home. The senior citizens will enjoy watching birds and squirrels gobble up your handiwork!

133

SAVE IT!

Is the wilderness around you vanishing? You can help stop the destruction!

What You'll Need: Notebook paper, envelope, pencil, stamp

Is there a wetland in your hometown? An old-growth forest? A rare bird nesting site? Is it safe, or is it in danger of being turned into a housing development? The Center for Children's Environmental Literature can help. Write for special suggestions on how to save wilderness areas in your own hometown. Then get busy putting the suggestions into action. Write to: Center for Children's Environmental Literature, P.O. Box 5995, Washington, DC 20016.

CELEBRATE GRANDPARENTS

In 1978, President Jimmy Carter proclaimed that National Grandparent's Day would be celebrated every year on the first Sunday after Labor Day.

RECYCLING ROUND-UP

Don't wait for recycling to come to your neighborhood—start some yourself!

What You'll Need: Large plastic trash bags, large cardboard boxes, magazine pictures, glue

Has your neighborhood started a recycling program? If not, why not start one of your own? Decorate large cardboard boxes, such as fruit or moving boxes, with phrases about recycling or pictures of pop cans. Give the boxes to trusted friends and neighbors, and ask them to keep their empty soda cans in their boxes. Collect the cans in large plastic garbage bags each week. Check your Yellow Pages to find your local recycling center. Turn in the bags of soda cans for a few cents weekly profit.

READ SOMEONE HAPPY

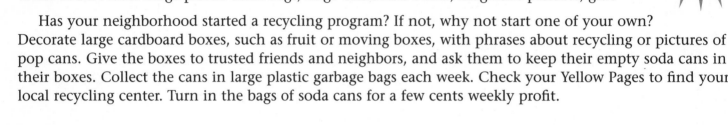

Reading to a friend can heal the heart.

What You'll Need: Your favorite picture books

Thousands of kids wind up confined to hospital beds every year as a result of serious illnesses or injuries. You can help cheer up sick kids and encourage their parents: Volunteer to read your favorite picture books to hospitalized children. Check with your local hospital's volunteer coordinator to find out when your talents might come in handy. Remember to keep your choice of books cheerful and encouraging. Laughter is often the very best medicine. You might also want to consider donating your old picture books to your local children's hospital.

PET PARADE

Share your pets with people less fortunate.

What You'll Need: Your pet, your pet's leash or carrier box

One of the things homeless people and senior citizens in assisted living facilities miss most are their pets. You and your pet can give them a few moments of furry fun. Make sure all your pet's shots are up to date (and make sure your pet is good with groups of strangers—you'll need your parents' okay for this). Then call your local homeless shelter or senior citizens group home to see if it's okay for you to drop by with an adult—and your pet! Once you arrive, move from room to room, just saying hello. Be prepared to talk about your pet—how long you've you had it, what it likes to eat, what it's named, things like that.

REACH OUT—BUT WHERE?

Hoping to reach out to the elderly but don't know where to look?
Check in your local telephone company's Yellow Pages under
"senior living" or "assisted living."

ICE WATER WELCOME

137

Let your city road crews know you appreciate their hard work.

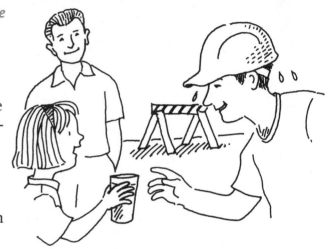

What You'll Need: Paper cups, ice water

Every summer it happens—hardworking road crews gather early in the morning and work until the end of the day. They repair cracks, fill potholes, and sometimes resurface the road. It's their job, and they're paid to keep your streets safe. But it's thirsty work. Why not offer them a welcome relief the next time they work near you? If your parents say it's okay, offer the street crews a clean paper cup full of ice-cold water. It's a thank you they won't soon forget. Remember, be sure to ask your parents before you approach anyone you don't know!

GIFT OF GIVING

138

Give the ability to give (the greatest gift of all).

What You'll Need: Beads, key chains, ribbon, miscellaneous gift goodies; bag or box; paper and pencil (optional)

Nothing feels better than the chance to give a heartfelt gift. So why not give a less fortunate person that opportunity? Gather together materials, such as beads, ribbons, key chains, colorful paper, glue, and fabric paints. Bag or box them up as a craft kit, and ask your local YMCA, Salvation Army, or social services offices to help you give them to people who will appreciate them most. Write your own instructions for specific crafts, or leave it up to the gift giver's imagination.

139 BACKYARD BIRD RESCUE

Birds get hungry, too—and you can help feed them!

What You'll Need: Disposable pie pans, string, scissors, birdseed, sharp implement for punching holes

When winter blows into town, thousands of birds fly out. For the few that remain, these easy-to-make bird feeders could mean the difference between life and death. Gather disposable pie pans, 3 equal-length pieces of string for each pan, and some birdseed to help keep birds' tiny tummies well fed. Have an adult help you punch holes in the outer edges of the pie pans. To place the holes correctly, imagine the pie pan is a clock face, and punch the holes at the 4, 8, and 12 o'clock positions. Feed 1 end of a string through a hole from the top of the pan to the bottom, and tie a sturdy knot on the bottom side. Repeat with the other strings and holes. Now tie the ends of the strings together at the top of the pan. Repeat the process with the other pie pans. Fill the feeders with birdseed, and have an adult help you hang them from a high branch (safe from neighborhood cats).

JAVA BIRDS

Did you know some migratory birds are crazy about coffee grounds? It's true, according to the Smithsonian Migratory Bird Center, in Washington, DC.

HALLOWEEN HELLO

140

Cheerful holiday greetings can make all seasons bright.

What You'll Need: Tiny pumpkins, permanent markers, ribbon

Holidays can be lonely occasions for some people. Special decorated pumpkins can add a cheerful little "boo!" to a lonely person's Halloween. Buy tiny pumpkins from your local grocery store or produce stand. Decorate each of them with cheerful, smiling faces and curls of brightly colored ribbon on the stems. Pass them out to less fortunate families and senior citizens in your neighborhood. Your local police department or YMCA can help distribute them, making sure they land in households that really need some holiday cheer. For holiday cheer throughout the year, make decorated evergreen branches, colored eggs, paper shamrocks, and other seasonal symbols.

SAYING HI
How do you say hello in other languages? *Hola:* Spanish. *Guten Tag:* German. *Bonjour:* French.

141

ART FOR SENIORS

Brighten a senior's world with your art!

What You'll Need: Paper, crayons, cardboard, large envelope, stamps

Many senior citizens find themselves in rest homes far from their own kids and grandkids. You can help brighten their days with a splash of color—bright and lively artwork only you can give. Draw and color your favorite scene—anything from animals to airplanes. Add your first name and your age. Glue your artwork to cardboard, and mail it off to a nearby home for the elderly. If you can share art once a month, your gift will keep on giving. If you can enlist your entire class to join in the fun, you'll inspire dozens of smiles and warm feelings.

HOMELESS HELPERS

142

Helping the homeless will help you feel good, too!

What You'll Need: Clearance aisle toiletries, prepackaged food, bag, markers

Helping the homeless isn't always easy, but handing over a thoughtful bag of essentials will show you care. Save your money to buy clearance aisle samples of lotion, soap, shampoo, etc. (about 50 cents each). Put those items along with a fresh, prepackaged snack in a paper bag (decorate the bag, if you like). Ask your local Salvation Army, church, or police department for advice on the best ways to share your gifts.

ICE PATROL

Sidewalk ice can be a serious danger for the elderly. You can help keep them safe.

What You'll Need: Cat litter, sand, rock salt, bucket

Winter snowfall means fun to most kids—sledding, snowball fights, and frosty activities galore. But to senior citizens, winter weather means icy sidewalks and all the danger that goes with them. If you have elderly people in your neighborhood, do a weekly ice patrol to help keep them safe. If you find a patch of stubborn ice on the sidewalk that just won't go away, ask your neighbor if you can sprinkle it with a mix of sand, rock salt, and cat litter. The rock salt will help melt the ice. The cat litter will soak up the frosty water. And the sand will help keep the ice from being slippery until the whole process kicks into action. But don't forget to ask permission first!

LONG LIVES
The average American now lives to be 75 years old—or older.

SECRET SANTA

144

Your old toys could be new treasures for someone special.

What You'll Need: Old toys, tape, glue, cleaning supplies, ribbon, construction or notebook paper

Is your room overflowing with toys and stuffed animals you've outgrown? Why not clean them up and give them to children less fortunate? Tape and glue torn game pieces, wash and disinfect soiled action figures, wash older stuffed animals inside a pillowcase in a washing machine. Attach a friendly little note with ribbon to each toy, and donate them to your local homeless shelter or YMCA. Also, don't forget well-known drives for new toys, such as Toys for Tots, when it comes time to share your spirit of giving!

145

YARDS OF HELPFULNESS

Help good feelings grow by cleaning up a neighbor's yard.

What You'll Need: Lawn mower, rake, weed trimmer, work gloves, trash bags, ice water

Is your neighbor disabled? Overworked? Sick? Ask if you can help by taking care of some of the yard work. Once they say it's okay, why not mow the lawn? Rake the leaves? Pull those ugly weeds? Not good with yard tools? Volunteer to baby-sit your neighbor's children as they do the difficult work. Offer to wash their dishes to free up a little extra time. Do what you can to grow some neighborly smiles and prove you care. Don't forget to bring a big bottle of ice water with you when you volunteer; yard clean-up can be hot and thirsty work.

STENCIL TILES

These cheerful ceramics will lift spirits and hearts.

What You'll Need: Tile, stencil, glass and tile paint, clear gloss, paintbrush

Making lovely tile works of art is an easy way to please friends and family or cheer up less fortunate strangers. Buy craft tiles (about $1 each) at your local hobby or craft store. Decorate them with cheerful designs using a stencil and tile paint. (Have an adult read the paint label for precautions—are paints nontoxic and do they need good air circulation for fumes? Always have an adult help you follow the label instructions!) Allow tiles to dry, then apply a thin layer of clear gloss to protect your hard work. Give the finished artwork as gifts to people you love. Or ask your local hospice to be sure they wind up in the hands of people who need a little cheering up. The tiles could also be used as coasters.

THE POWER OF ONE
Does every vote count? In 1845, one vote made Texas a state. In 1868,
a single vote saved President Andrew Johnson from being thrown out of office.
In 1923, one vote gave Adolf Hitler leadership of the Nazi party.
Yes, every vote can make a difference!

GREAT GAMES

The hard part of the day is done. Now it's play time!
You can play many of the games in this chapter on your own;
others are great for groups.
Get creative and come up with your own variations.
You might even be inspired to create
original games from scratch!

147 · ONE PEG AT A TIME

A pegboard solitaire game—or duel—is fast-paced fun.

What You'll Need: Thin poster board, graph paper and glue stick
(optional), pencil, ruler, pushpins, container to hold pushpins, thick
stack of newspaper

Plan out any grid design you like. Just make sure it has an odd
number of dots or places where lines cross each other. If
you're using graph paper, cut it to the desired shape and
glue to the poster board. Lay the board on newspaper and stick
a pushpin into every dot or line intersection. Leave one space
open in the center. The object of the game is to "jump" pins
over each other and remove them one at a time, as in
checkers. The catch: You must end with the last pin in the
center space. For a duel, have a friend make a board also. Then
challenge each other to see who finishes first.

PICTOMINOES

148

Custom-make your dominoes with pictures instead of dots.

What You'll Need: Index cards in white or pastel shades, ink pads, 6 small rubber stamps

Count out 28 index cards. On the blank side of each card, draw a line through the middle from one long side to the other. Take one of the ink stamps and make prints on 1 side of 4 of the index cards. Do the same with the rest of the ink stamps. This should leave you with 4 random spaces that are blank. That's OK; these are wild spaces. Play with your "pictominoes" as if they had dots, only match up the pictures instead!

JAZZY JIGSAWS

149

You can also mail these nifty jigsaws to family or friends as surprises.

What You'll Need: Thin poster board; pencil; photo, magazine picture or drawing; glue stick; scissors

Start small at first, to perfect your puzzle-making prowess. Cut the poster board to your desired finished size. Next, cut a photo or picture to the size of the poster board. Glue the photo or picture to the board with the glue stick. On the backside of the poster board, about 1 inch from the left edge, draw a zigzag line from top to bottom with a pencil. Draw a similar line 1 inch away from that, and continue across the board. Now draw zigzag lines from side to side, about 1 inch away from each other. Cut along each line. Turn each puzzle piece face up. Put together your own designer jigsaw creation!

THE GREAT ADVENTURE

150

Bring your favorite action hero or heroine to life.

What You'll Need: Action figure, heavy poster board, pencil, thick black marker, paints and paintbrushes or colored markers, clear adhesive vinyl, thin poster board, scissors, game pieces from other board games or colored glass pebbles, die

Come up with an adventure for your favorite hero or heroine action figure. Give him or her a goal to reach and several funny obstacles along the way. Sketch in the starting point in a corner of the poster board and the end in the opposite corner. Draw scattered obstacles in the middle. Draw a path, with marked spaces big enough for your game pieces, between the starting point and the end. Mark some spaces "hazard." Finish coloring in the board with markers or paints. Let dry. Cover with clear adhesive vinyl for lots of use. Use the thin poster board to make hazard cards to turn over when you land on one of these spaces. Name the hazard and the penalties, such as "Lose a turn," "Go back 2 spaces," "Start over," etc. Grab your game pieces, roll the die, and begin the adventure!

Action Jobs

Looking for a career in adventure? Consider being a fighter pilot, a police detective, or a competitive hockey player. Or report on all these adventurers as a journalist.

PENCIL ME IN

This game is tougher than you think.

What You'll Need: 20 unsharpened pencils, flat surface

Scatter the pencils on a tabletop, with several lying across each other. The object of the game is to remove 1 pencil at a time without making any of the other pencils move. It can be done! The game ends when a pencil moves. Hint: You can use a pencil that's already been removed to try to push or flip out a pencil that's still in the pile. This is great fun to play alone, but it is also lots of fun with friends!

WHAT IS THAT?

This guessing game makes everyone use more than their sense of sight! This is the nondigusting version. You could do a gross-out version with a large bowl hidden inside a cardboard box.

What You'll Need: Hat or stocking cap; 3 differently textured objects that are hard, rough, and silky; pencil; paper

Put all 3 objects into the hat. In a separate room, have each player reach into the hat (without looking) and try to guess what each object is. After everyone has had a try, meet together in a room and have everyone write down the mystery objects. The winners are those who guess correctly. For a more gross-out version of this game, put 3 bowls in a cardboard box covered with black cloth. Place peeled grapes; cold, cooked noodles; and cut-up gelatin in the bowls. Now have your friends guess what they are touching! Yucky!

153 FOX AND HOUNDS

Who will outfox whom? Play the game to find out!

What You'll Need: A group of people, the larger the better; deck of cards

Everyone sits in a circle. Remove all the face cards from a deck of cards except for 1 joker. Choose a person to be the game leader. Count out as many cards as there are people playing, except for the game leader, making sure to include the joker. The game leader deals out the cards face down to the other players. Whoever gets the joker is the fox. After the cards have been passed out, they are collected again. Now the game leader instructs the group, or "hounds," to "fall asleep" by bowing their heads and closing their eyes. Only the fox stays "awake" so the game leader can identify him or her. The game leader calls for the hounds to "awaken." The group plays the game in rounds, eliminating 1 person from the game at a time.

When the hounds "awaken," the players stare closely at each others' eyes and suggest one or more people they believe to be the fox. When they decide on a person to question, he or she must tell the group why he or she couldn't be the fox. If the group believes that person, they choose another until they find a person they decide to eliminate. Meanwhile, while everyone is staring at each other, the fox carefully winks at someone (without being seen by the others) and eliminates them. That person waits a few seconds, and then announces, "I've just been outfoxed."

The game leader calls for the hounds to "fall asleep" again, and everyone except the fox and the eliminated players bow their heads and close their eyes. Once someone is eliminated, they can remain and watch the rest of the game, but they may not speak at any time or give clues about the fox's identity. Play continues until 1 person is left—either the fox or a hound. The hounds win the game if they manage to find the fox in this manner before he or she outfoxes them.

ROADBLOCK!

154

This is HUGE fun and a great way to get to know people.

What You'll Need: Group of people, the larger the better; living room furniture; 1 less chair or seat on the couch than the number of people playing

One person stands in the middle of the group and tells one thing about himself or herself, such as "My name begins with A." Then everyone for whom that statement is true—in this case, anyone else whose name begins with A—jumps up and dashes for a different empty seat (including the person in the middle). It can't be right next to the seat you just had. If only 1 other person jumps up, they are next to stand in the middle. If no one jumps up, the same person must tell something new about himself or herself. Here's the tricky part—no item can ever be repeated. If you can't think of something new, yell, "Roadblock!" Then everyone must jump up, grab another seat, and avoid being the person left standing.

155

TURKEY IN THE STRAWS

This game is tricky because straws don't have flat sides!

What You'll Need: Large, empty margarine tub; drinking straws; plastic cup

Lay several drinking straws crosswise on the margarine tub. Now balance a cup, turned upside down, on the straws. Each player takes a turn removing 1 straw at a time. Whoever pulls the straw that makes the cup fall down is the "turkey." He or she must gobble out loud! Practice this game by yourself—you won't be the turkey next time you play with friends!

STOP!

What is the most common cause of real-life roadblocks? Sobriety checkpoints (where police stop drivers to see if they've been drinking), according to most law enforcement officials. Drinking and driving definitely don't mix.

BALLOON TOSS

156

Test your aim in this cool point-scoring game.

What You'll Need: Bag of regular party balloons; metallic balloons, 4 of each color per player; plastic or paper funnel; flour; heavy poster board; big cardboard box; coffee mug; jumbo marker; scissors; masking tape

Very carefully (and with permission, so you get to do this again!), slip a regular balloon inside a metallic balloon. Blow into the balloons to straighten out the inside balloon. Next, stretch the neck of the double balloon over the narrow end of the funnel, and fill the inside balloon almost full with flour. Have an adult help you securely tie off the end. Make 4 balloons for each player—with each player having different colors. Find a piece of heavy poster board big enough to fit over a big cardboard box. Lay the poster board on the floor and trace around a coffee mug near the top center. This is the top of a "pyramid." Trace 2 more circles centered underneath the first circle. Leave about 4 inches between rows. Trace 3 more circles centered under the 2 circles. Cut out the circles. Over the top circle, mark "10" points. Over each of the 2 circles in the middle, mark "5" points. Over the remaining circles, mark "1" point. Lay the poster board over the box, and tape the edges down with masking tape. Stand back from the box about 5 to 7 feet. Play by yourself, or have friends over for a challenge match. Players take turns throwing the balloons into the holes to score points. Start tossing balloons!

A BALLOON FIRST

One of the first hot-air balloons rose 6,000 feet into the air on June 5, 1783. It was made of linen and paper and was constructed by brothers Joseph and Aetienne Montgolfier in Annonay, France.

157

ALL MIXED UP

Let's see how your story stacks up!

What You'll Need: Sunday comics, scissors

Find your favorite comic strip, and cut apart the story frames. Mix up the pieces, and try to put them back in the correct order. Here's a goofy challenge: Lay them out in front of your friends in random order. Now have them try to make up a story that makes sense out of the scrambled pictures! Or show them the frames in the correct order, but leave off the last frame and see what kind of ending they come up with.

HORSE

158

This kind of "horse" can be played during bad weather, too.

What You'll Need: Die

Just as in the basketball version of "horse," whoever makes a successful throw must be copied by all the others or they earn a letter from the word "horse." Decide who will throw the die first. Whatever number lands faceup must be matched by the other players. Whoever successfully matches the first throw leads the second round. If nobody matches the throw, the first player throws the next round. The players who did not match the throw in the first round earn the letter "h." On the second throw they don't match, players earn the letter "o," and so on until someone spells the word "horse." When a player can spell "horse," the game is over.

ARCHES

159

Try shooting marbles through a funhouse!

What You'll Need: 2 empty shoe boxes, scissors, glue, pencil, poster paints, paintbrush, marbles

The object is to build a marble-shooting path through arches to score points. Remove the lids from both shoe boxes. Leave one box intact. Cut down the 4 corners of the second box. Flatten the 2 short ends into "tongues." In one short end of the uncut box, cut out 2 small arches, about 2 inches wide and 2 inches tall. Make sure there's an inch between the arches. In the other short end of the box, cut out 3 smaller arches. Make sure there's space between each arch and between the arches and the sides of the box. Think of a design to paint around each arch, such as a monster mouth or a bunny mouth. Paint the outside of the box on the side with the 2 arches, and on the inside of the box with the side with the 3 arches. Let dry.

Above the 2 arches paint "5" points and "10" points. Paint higher point amounts above each of the 3 arches. Glue 1 of the "tongues" of the cut-open box underneath the end of the box with 2 arches. Break down a short end of 1 of the lids, and glue it under the end with 3 arches to create a lip that will catch the marbles. Now, get shooting. Place a marble on the edge of the tongue, and flick it through the arches with thumb and forefinger. The number of points you earn depends on which holes the marble goes through. Play 5 rounds of marble-shooting fun!

MARBLE ORIGINS

Some of the earliest marbles were actually damaged beads passed on to Egyptian children for games.

MARBLE TOSS

160

Playing this game is easy. Scoring high is not so easy!

What You'll Need: Clean, dry egg carton; black crayon; five marbles; large beach towel (optional)

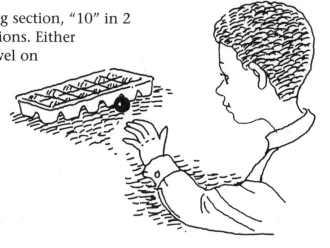

With the black crayon, write "15" in the bottom of 1 egg section, "10" in 2 sections, "5" in 3 sections, and "1" in the remaining 6 sections. Either play this game on a rug or carpet or spread out a beach towel on the floor. Lay the carton on the rug or beach towel, and stand about 5 feet away. Toss your marbles, 1 at a time, into the egg carton, and add up your score. When you think you're getting pretty good, challenge your friend to a game! The highest score wins.

161

TRIANGULATION

In a race of triangles, who will make the most?

What You'll Need: Sheet of white, unlined paper; ruler; pencils

This is a game for 2 or 3 players. With the ruler and a pencil, the first player makes a small triangle in the center of the paper. The player's score for that turn is 1, since 1 triangle was formed. The second player is allowed to make 3 lines with the ruler and pencil. They may make the lines anywhere they like. If they make them around the first triangle, with 2 sides overlapping 2 sides of the first triangle, their score is 2; 1 for the triangle they made and 1 for the triangle within the triangle they just made. By overlapping lines, they also set up an interesting opportunity for multiple scores in the future. Play continues with each player making 3 moves and scoring according to the number of triangles contained in the triangle just formed. The game ends when players run out of room on the paper.

THE HOUSE THAT CARDS BUILT

Sure you can build a house, but you have to get cards from your own suit first!

What You'll Need: Standard deck of cards, large table or floor, 4 players

Before play starts, each of the players must pick a suit to call his or her own: hearts, diamonds, clubs, or spades. Pull the jokers from the deck, and deal out all the cards to the players. The game is played in rounds. If any of the players have 3 cards of their own suit right after they are dealt, they may put the 3 cards together to begin to build their house. Try holding 2 cards upright and placing a card flat on top of them. In the next round, each player passes 1 card to their right. If a player already has another suit card or just gained 1, they may add it to their house. If they don't have another suit card, they wait until the next round. The rounds continue until someone's house falls down. Then that player's cards are dealt out to the remaining players. This is repeated until only 1 house is standing—the house belonging to the winner of the game!

HAT TRICK

163

This one only sounds easy!

What You'll Need: Standard deck of cards, hat with stiff sides or small empty garbage can

This is a game for 4 players. Divide the deck into the 4 different suits, and give a suit to each player. Set aside the jokers. Lay the hat on the floor, brim up. Stand back about 7 feet. Take turns tossing cards into the hat. When all the cards have been tossed, set aside the ones that missed the hat. Each player counts the number of cards in his or her suit that landed in the hat. If there is a tie, those players play another round to determine a winner. This is also a fun activity to play by yourself—you can practice your skills for the next time your friends come to visit!

164

3-D TIC-TAC-TOE

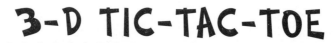

Here's an old favorite made into a brain-bender.

What You'll Need: Sheet of white paper, pencil

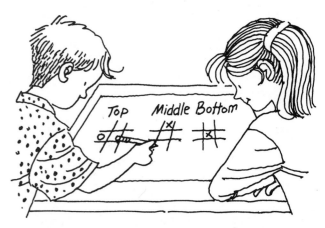

This is a game for 2 players. Draw 3 tic-tac-toe grids side by side. Label them "top," "middle," and "bottom." The goal is still to make 3 of your own marks in a row. However, you can now score a win by placing a mark in the upper left of the top level, 1 in the center of the middle level, and 1 in the lower right of the bottom level. The same goes for vertical or horizontal lines. Try playing fast—it's trickier than it looks. Once you've mastered 3 levels, try 4, 5, 6, or more levels. Remember, there must be as many rows across and down in each grid as there are levels played on. For instance, if you play on 5 levels, each grid must have 5 rows across and down.

CHICKEN IN THE BARNYARD

Play smart and think fast. You don't want to be the chicken!

What You'll Need: Standard deck of cards; spoons or dice, one fewer than the number of players

Up to 13 people may play. Since this game is played with sets of 4 similar cards, choose as many sets as there are players. For instance, if there are 6 players, use all the cards ranked ace through 6. Place spoons or dice in the middle of the table, one fewer than the number playing. Deal the cards face down. The goal is to get a set of 4 cards of the same rank (for example, 4 queens). Pick 1 card to discard, lay it face down, and slide it to the player on your left. Pick up the card passed to you from the player on your right. Keep picking up and passing cards quickly until someone gets a set of 4 of the same cards. He or she then grabs a spoon or die from the center—trying to do it without making a big ruckus. As soon as someone does this, everybody else needs to grab for a spoon, too. Whoever comes up empty earns a letter in the word "chicken." The game ends when a player can spell the word. He or she then must cluck like a chicken!

DOMINO DUPLEX

Patience, not speed, wins this game.

What You'll Need: Standard set of dominoes

The object is to build a house, 1 player and 1 domino at a time. The first player lays a domino down on its side. The next player adds another domino in such a way as to start building a house. Keep in mind that you will have to lay dominoes on their long or short sides so that they stick up to make walls. Players take turns adding dominoes to build up the building—it gets tricky pretty quickly! The game is over when the first domino falls down. An alternative is to play this game by yourself, each time trying to add more dominoes. Keep track of how many you add. You can also time yourself; see how many you can place before the timer goes off!

WHAT'S IN A ROOM?

167

Now you see it, now you don't. What do you remember?

What You'll Need: Paper, pencils

This game is very simple and fun. Lead the group into a room with lots of things in it, both big and small. Give them 2 minutes to memorize what they see in the room. Then lead them back into the party room, and give them 2 more minutes to write down everything they remember seeing. Whoever remembers the most things correctly wins.

DYNAMIC DIGITS

Numbers are fascinating—and they are everywhere!
So much we do depends on working with numbers,
including playing music, cooking, and even playing board games.
So strap on your thinking cap, get ready to count,
and let's have some fun with numbers!

TRIANGLE TREAT

168

Make a three-sided sensation for mathematical fun.

What You'll Need: Card stock, scissors

Triangles are 3-sided wonders. Can anyone get enough of them? If you love these geometric gems, why not try this artful game? Cut colorful card stock into dozens of tiny triangles. Now arrange the triangles into delightful shapes and designs on the floor, a table, or your desk. Can you make squares from triangles? Patterns? Designs? There's only one way to find out. Get going with a friend for twice the 3-sided fun.

TIC-TAC-TOADS

169

*Get hopping on **this great new game** of three in a row!*

What You'll Need: Colored paper, colored markers or crayons, scissors, plain paper, envelope, clear adhesive vinyl (optional)

Give tic-tac-toe a hoppy new boost by making the traditional X's and O's color-coded frogs. Draw and cut out 2 sets of 9 paper frogs. Cut out 1 set from green paper and the other from blue paper (or any color you like best). Draw a standard tic-tac-toe game board as shown in the illustration. Be sure to slip your leaping game pieces and board in an envelope for safekeeping between games. To make your game extra sturdy, cover the frog game pieces and playing board with clear adhesive vinyl.

170

RACE WITH TIME

*Learn to **tell time** in no time at all with this fun face-off.*

What You'll Need: Paper plates, black markers, colored paper, scissors, paper brads, scorepad, pencil

Learning to tell time is easy and fun, thanks to this game. Each player makes their own clock face out of a paper plate, complete with moving minute and hour hands. Mark the paper plate with the hours, as on a clock. Cut out a big hand and a small hand from colored paper. Attach the hands in the middle of the plate with a paper brad. Now you are ready to play the game! Ask an adult or older friend to shout out times, such as 1:15 or 2:45. The first player to move the hands to show the correct time on his or her clock face wins the round and 5 points on the score pad. The first person to reach 50 points wins the game. Add more to the game: Score extra points for the player who can name an appropriate activity for the time (such as lunch or bedtime) along with marking the time on the clock.

BEANBAG BUNDLES

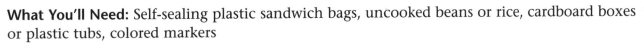

171

Make your own magic with this bean-bundling fun!

What You'll Need: Self-sealing plastic sandwich bags, uncooked beans or rice, cardboard boxes or plastic tubs, colored markers

Fill self-sealing plastic sandwich bags half-full of beans (pinto, lima, even uncooked peas or rice will do). Double bag your beans, and squeeze out excess air—they'll be less likely to spill or break. Decorate cardboard boxes or plastic tubs with brightly colored numbers. The higher the number, the farther away the tub should be from your starting mark. Now toss your beanbags into the tubs, and keep track of how many land in each numbered container. Add the scores for each container, then add the scores for all the containers together. Next, have other players take a turn throwing the beanbags into the containers. The player with the highest score wins. You can compete against your own high score if you're playing alone.

GO FISH!

172

Fish for higher scores every time you net these colorful swimmers.

What You'll Need: Colored paper, scissors, paper clips, large cardboard box, magnet, string, yardstick or dowel, colored markers

Cut out 2 dozen 3-inch fish from different colors of paper (the simpler the fish, the easier the fishing). Slip a paper clip on the end of each fish, and toss them into an empty cardboard box. Tie a magnet to an end of a 24-inch string, and dangle it from the end of a yardstick or dowel. As you cast your line into the box, you'll reel in colorful fish time and time again. Assign each color of fish a point value; red is 1 point, blue is 3 points, green is 6 points, etc. Then, as you catch fish, keep adding up your score. For extra fun, decorate the outside of the box with a creative seascape—sunken treasure, flippered flounders, friendly mermaids, and more.

DIME A MINUTE

173

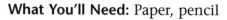

Talk is cheap when your phone calls are local. But try playing this game of "what if."

What You'll Need: Paper, pencil

Everyone's heard the "dime a minute" telephone company ads. How much would your telephone talk cost if local calls were also 10 cents a minute? Keep track of your telephone time for 1 week. Multiply the minutes by 10 cents. If you get paid for jobs around the house, what would you have to do to earn that much money?

174 WATER CLOCK ESTIMATION

Use water to tell time and also to test your sense of how long things take!

What You'll Need: Paper cup, straight pin, cylinder-shaped jar, pin, water, pitcher, permanent marker, digital clock

Begin by making your time-telling tool, a water clock. To make the clock, pierce a hole in the bottom of the paper cup with a straight pin. Set the cup in the jar so it rests in the rim—the bottom of the cup should not touch the bottom of the jar. With a digital clock or a watch with a second hand nearby, fill the cup with water. Using a permanent marker, record the water level reached at 1-minute intervals on the outside of the jar. Mark off each minute for 15 minutes. Then empty the cup and the jar, and get ready to use the water clock for estimation challenges. How many minutes does it take you to brush your teeth? How long does it take to make a peanut butter and jelly sandwich? Or to do 25 jumping jacks? Make an estimate, fill the glass with water, do the task, and test out your estimate. You can also make another clock for tracking time for longer periods. Use a larger jar, and this time, mark the water level reached at 15-minute intervals. (You might want to use a kitchen timer to remind you when to record the 15-minute intervals!)

TIME TO TELL

For more than 22 centuries, human beings have used sundials to tell time. Considering most were made of stone or copper, they wouldn't have made very good wristwatches!

TV TAG WITH NUMBERS

175

Count on this game for television fun by the numbers.

What You'll Need: Blank paper, TV, remote control, pens or pencils

Want to study your numbers and watch your favorite television shows? Tune in to a game of TV Tag. Using your remote control, flip through the channels until you see the number 1 on the screen (either as a number or spelled out). It could be in an address, an advertisement, or a cartoon or live-action program. Once you score the 1, move on to finding a 2, 3, 4, and so on. The first player to find the numbers 1 through 10 is the winner. If you are playing alone, try to beat your own best time.

176

BUTTON, BUTTON

Tossing colorful buttons adds up to number-loving fun!

What You'll Need: Paper, colored markers or crayons, ruler, 24 buttons (12 of one color, 12 of another), scorepad

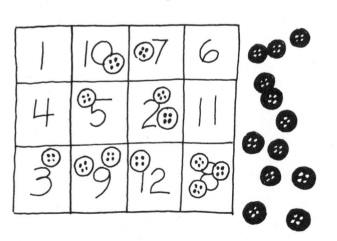

Using a blank piece of paper, make a game board with 12 same-size squares. Randomly label each square with the numbers 1 to 12. Once your game board is complete, place it on a table. Place your 12 colored buttons next to the board, then flick each button with your fingernail onto the board. Add up your score based on where your buttons landed (for example, if all 12 of your buttons landed on the 10 square, give yourself 120 points). Make a note of your score on the score pad. Pick up your buttons, and watch your friend flick his or her buttons. You can also play against yourself to better your own score.

ENLARGE IT!

177

Draw an outline of a pair of scissors, a watch, your hand, or something else you commonly look at, then blow it up in size to see it in a whole new way!

What You'll Need: Object that can be outlined, paper, pencil, ruler

Choose an object (or several) to blow up. Place the object on a piece of paper and trace its outline. After the outline is drawn, remove the object, and, using a ruler, draw grid lines on the paper over your outline. To make a grid, measure and mark each side of the paper at regular intervals (such as every ½ inch). Then, again using the ruler, draw vertical and horizontal lines across the paper, starting at the marks you made. Now, using a much bigger paper, create a bigger grid for the enlarged picture. Use mural paper or tape together several large sheets of paper to make giant paper. Then make a grid with lines 2, 3, or 4 inches apart (depending on how big the big paper is). Copy what's in each square in the small grid into the matching square of the large grid, enlarging it to fit into the larger space. When you're done, you'll have a blow-up of the object you've outlined.

TELLING THEM APART

Identical twins are perhaps the world's most noticeable pairs. But not everything about them is duplicated. According to Los Angeles forensics experts, the perfect resemblance stops when it comes to fingerprints.

BY THE NUMBERS

178

Play hopscotch with a 12-way twist.

What You'll Need: Chalk, sidewalk

This version of hopscotch will have you jumping for joy. Make a grid of 12 squares, each 2×2 feet, on the sidewalk. Number the squares 1 to 12 (you don't have to number them in any particular order—but be sure numbers aren't more than 1 row away from the previous number). Now hop on 1 foot from square 1 to square 2, square 3, and so on. Each player's turn ends when he or she accidentally steps out of a square or lands out of sequence. No one misses the easy way? Turn up the heat. Make them put their hands behind their backs and repeat the process. Still no flubs? Try jumping to only even-numbered or odd-numbered squares.

MONUMENTAL NUMBER FACTS

179

Collect extremely enormous and staggering number facts.

What You'll Need: Pencil, paper, reference materials (encyclopedia, newspaper, almanac)

Set out on a number fact search—write down as many facts as you can that include large numbers. Here are some big-number facts to begin with: People have about 100,000 hairs growing on their heads. There are 525,600 minutes in a year. There are 31,536,000 seconds in a year! One good acre of land can have anywhere from 50,000 to 1,000,000 worms underground. There are more than 800,000 species of insects in the world. There are about 8,000,000 words in the English language. Now, add to the list. How many more big-number facts can you find? Use an encyclopedia, an almanac, online resources, a newspaper, and any other fact finders available! Write down your big-number facts, and keep adding to the collection.

TWO BY TWO

It takes two to make a pair and pairs to win this game.

What You'll Need: Paper pad, pens or pencils

Ever notice how many things come in pairs, naturally? Think about it—2 eyes, 2 legs, 2 feet, 2 shoes. The list goes on and on. How far depends on you. Take a walk around your house, your yard, your neighborhood. How many things can you find that seem to come in pairs? Run out of 2s? Look for natural 4s or dozens or hundreds. Compare your list with a friend. This also makes a great party game for teams.

ADD A CARD

Card-carrying math wizards can win this in a flash!

What You'll Need: Playing cards, score pad, pens or pencils

Looking for a new take on adding numbers? It's in the cards! Draw 2 regular playing cards from a standard deck, and deal 2 to your friend. Whoever correctly adds up the combined face value of their cards first wins the round and the point. The player with the most points at the end of the deck wins. Face cards and aces are always worth 10 points. For an added challenge, put a time limit on the simple addition.

COUNTING, ROMAN STYLE

Think our number system is difficult? Try counting from I to X.
The ancient Roman number system used combinations of I, V, X, L, C, D, and
M to make every number in the book.

DOUBLE UP

Fill 'er up—then fill 'er up again! And again. And again.

What You'll Need: Measuring cups, bucket, water, paper pad, pen or pencil

Want an easy way to understand multiplication and division? Double up! Use a measuring cup to fill a bucket with water. Start with ¼ cup. Keep track of how many ¼ cups it takes to fill your bucket to the brim. Write the number down on a paper pad. Now dump your bucket (in a plugged sink to recycle the water), and fill it up again, this time using a ½-cup measure. How many dips of the cup did it take to fill the bucket this time? Exactly half as many? If not, you spilled. Try it again with a 1-cup measure. You'll have a watery grasp on fractions in no time at all.

KITE HEIGHTS

Kite flying soars to new heights when you ask, "How high is high?"

What You'll Need: Kite, string, yardstick, colored markers

The next time you fly a kite, take steps to find out just how high it will rise. Before you launch your soaring beauty, mark your string in 10-foot stretches. Measure out 10 feet of string. Color it blue. Measure out the next 10 feet, and color it green. Make the next 10 feet of string red. Keep going with as much of the string as you have the patience to mark. Then launch your kite. Keep track of how many different colors slip through your hands, then multiply that number by 10. Hint: Make a note of how much string you tied onto your kite so you'll know how high it's gone when it comes to the end of its string.

SALAD TOSS

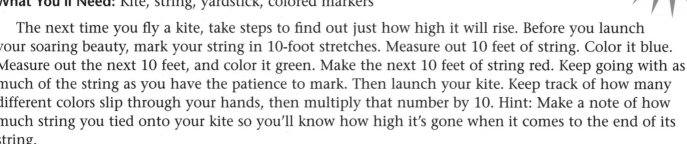

Toss up a vegetarian treat—lettuce have some fun!

What You'll Need: Colorful card stock, plastic bowls, black markers

Make paper salad bits from colorful card stock or lightweight cardboard. Try green paper lettuce leaves, red tomato slices, white onion cubes, orange carrot chunks. Divide players into 2 teams. Take turns sailing salad bits through the air, trying to land them in the large plastic bowls. The team with the most salad tossed on target wins. For an added challenge, assign each piece of salad a number value. Assign more points for smaller pieces that land in the bowls, fewer points for easier-to-toss lettuce leaves. Tally the totals to determine the winner. You can also play by yourself to keep improving your score!

HOW TALL IS THAT TREE?

185

Figure out the height of a tall tree without using a ladder!

What You'll Need: Pencil, paper, measuring tape

(You will need to know how tall you are to do the tree height calculations.) Using the measuring tape, measure the shadow of a tree on a sunny day. Write down the length of the tree's shadow. Then measure your own shadow (you might want a friend to help you with this part). If you are working alone, use 2 rocks as markers for measuring your own shadow. Place a rock on the ground. Stand so that the top of your shadow is touching the rock. Then place the second rock at your feet. Now measure the distance between the rocks. Write down the length of your shadow. Next, perform a calculation using the tree's shadow length, your shadow length, and your height. This calculation will tell you the tree's height. To calculate, divide the length of the tree's shadow by the length of your shadow. Next, multiply that number by your own height. Now you know how tall the tree is!

PENNY PYRAMID

Stack up your riches in a game that makes cents.

What You'll Need: Several hundred pennies

Set out a square of pennies 10 pennies long and 10 pennies wide. Then make a 8×8-penny square on top of the original square, leaving the outside edge only 1 penny high. Repeat the process with an 6×6-penny square, leaving the outside square 1 penny high, the next square 2 pennies high. Continue until the center 4 pennies are the highest, and then add a triangle of pennies to that layer. Add a single penny in the center to top off the pyramid. Can you figure out how many pennies you used? Be sure to wash your hands before and after you play.

COUNT ME IN!

Go on a numbers hunt, and see how high it takes you.

Here's an activity that will help you see the numbers that are around you all the time. Find something inside or outside the house that you see only 1 of. Now find something you see 2 of. Continue looking for 3 of something, 4 of something, and 5 of something. For example, you may only have 1 kitchen table, but 2 wall clocks, 3 TVs, 4 kitchen chairs, etc. See how high you can count! You might want to challenge a friend to see who can reach the highest number.

GEOMETRICAL TOOTHPICKS

See how many geometric shapes you can build using toothpicks and modeling clay.

What You'll Need: Plastic table covering, toothpicks, modeling clay

Cover your work surface with a plastic table covering. Use the modeling clay to attach the ends of the toothpicks together. Can you create a triangle? A square? A rectangle? What about a dodecahedron? Or a geodesic? Try altering the shapes by varying the number of toothpicks that intersect at the clay corners in each shape. More toothpicks intersecting at the clay corners in a shape will create larger and rounder shapes. Try making a shape with 3 toothpicks intersecting at each clay corner, another with 4, and another with 5! Use colored toothpicks to create more decorative geometric sculptures.

MYSTERIOUS TRIANGLE
The Bermuda Triangle, which is roughly 440,000 square miles, is off the coast of southeast Florida. Supposedly over 50 airplanes and boats have vanished from there without a trace.

ONE-TO-TEN

189

Create a one-to-ten book, and illustrate it with one-to-ten pictures.

What You'll Need: Paper, stapler, crayons or markers

To make the book, staple together 11 pieces of paper (the top sheet is the cover). Write a title on the cover, and then number each of the following spreads (the 2 pages that face each other) with the numbers 1 through 10. On each spread, draw a picture that corresponds to the number on the page. On spread 1, draw 1 thing. On spread 2, draw 2 items. On spread 3, draw 3 things, and so on. Create a theme for your book. For example, make a 1-to-10 book of animals, and choose a different animal for each spread (1 bear, 2 cats, 3 zebras, etc.). Or illustrate number facts about yourself. For instance, on the "1" spread, draw something you have 1 of (1 heart, 1 dog, or 1 toothbrush). On the "2" spread, draw something you have 2 of (2 feet, 2 hands, or 2 cats). Keep going!

190

PENCIL PATTERNS

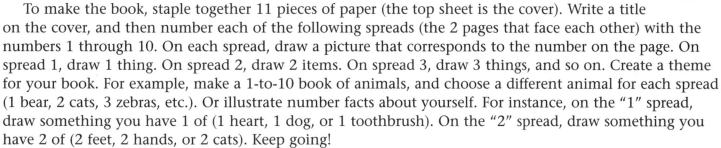

Pencil in some fun with the write designs.

What You'll Need: 24 unsharpened pencils, flat work space

Using 24 unsharpened pencils, you can experiment with designs and distinctive patterns. How many different arrangements can you make with all the erasers touching? How many unique shapes can you build with only 12 pencils? How long are the pencils when laid end to end to end? Can you stack pencils to make 3-dimensional designs? Anything goes in this pencil-pushing fun. If you don't have 24 pencils handy, try this activity with toothpicks.

STRETCH IT!

191

Test a few boundaries with this experiment in fun!

What You'll Need: Samples of flexible materials (cotton, licorice, knit fabrics, elastic, rubber bands), yardstick, paper, pens or pencils

How far can you stretch a rubber band? How far can you stretch a piece of elastic? How far can you stretch your favorite T-shirt? Find out with this fun experiment. Measure 5 ordinary items in their "normal" condition. Mark that measure on paper. Stretch those same items and record that measurement beside the original. Compare which of the 5 items stretched the most. Graph the results.

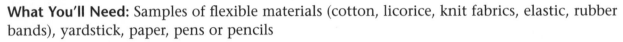

192

THE BIG FREEZE

Chill out to find what's what when it comes to things that freeze.

What You'll Need: Balloons, water, freezer, ruler or measuring tape, paper, pens or pencils

Have you ever slipped a full plastic drink bottle in the freezer at bedtime, only to find it cracked at the crack of dawn? It's a fact of physics—frozen things expand. To find out how much, try this chilly challenge. Fill 3 small balloons with water. Leave a little air space at the top of each balloon when you tie it off. Barely fill the first, then tie it. Double the water in the second balloon, and tie it. Triple the water of the first in the third balloon, and tie it. Measure the water balloons. Put all 3 in the freezer overnight. Measure the balloons again after they are frozen. Compare the results.

"GRID" AND BEAR IT

You only need to be able to count to 15 to play this game.

What You'll Need: Pencil, paper

Create your own numbers puzzle. Draw a grid that's 3 squares by 3 squares. Put a number from 1 to 9 in each square. Here's the catch: The numbers in each row have to add up to 15 in every direction—up and down, side to side, and diagonally. Can you find more than 1 way to make the puzzle work? Play this yourself or play it with a friend, competing to see who can be first to create a puzzle that adds up correctly. The answer is on the following page at the bottom, upside down.

SPECIAL DELIVERY

Yes! It's good news, but can you write it in code so prying eyes won't see the secret before your best friend reads it?

What You'll Need: Pencil, paper

Afraid that top-secret note you gave your friend in the hallway might fall into enemy hands? Secret codes to the rescue! The simplest way to make up a code is to assign each letter of the alphabet a certain number. For example, look at this code: A=1, B=5, C=9, D=13, E=17, and so on. Do you see how it works? Each letter takes a number that's 4 plus the number of the previous letter. Let your best friend in on your code, and use it to share confidential chat. Codes are also a great way to protect your diary entries from snooping siblings!

INTERSECTING CIRCLES

195

Here's a handy way to think about sorting and categories.

What You'll Need: Markers, paper, old magazines, scissors, glue

A Venn diagram is a diagram that demonstrates intersecting sets. To make a Venn diagram, draw 2 overlapping circles on a piece of paper. Cut out pictures from an old magazine to sort into groups. You might choose 1 kind of picture to start with, such as pictures of animals, clothing, toys, etc. Think of 2 different qualities you could use for sorting the pictures in your group. For example, you could sort many of the animal pictures into 2 groups: animals with tails and animals with spots. Or you might try to sort clothing pictures into clothing with pockets and clothing with buttons. Place 1 group of pictures in the first circle you've drawn and the other group in the other circle. Use the overlap section in the middle of the circles for pictures that fit both groups (animals that have tails and spots, clothing that has pockets and buttons). You've created a Venn diagram! Glue your pictures in place to complete the diagram. You can also try drawing and illustrating your own invented categories instead of using magazine pictures, sorting canceled stamps into Venn diagrams, or making a 3-circle Venn diagram with 3 categories that overlap!

CIRCLES, CIRCLES, CIRCLES!

John Venn (1834–1923) was a student of and then later became president of Caius College, Cambridge University, England. In Caius Hall at Cambridge University is a stained glass window that honors Venn. The stained glass is of three intersecting circles.

(Answer to "Grid" and Bear It: First row: 3 5 7; second row: 8 1 6; third row: 4 9 2.)

ARTFUL NUMBERS

Make a colorful collage of numbers cut out from magazine pictures.

196

What You'll Need: Old magazines, scissors, construction paper, glue

To start, look through old magazines and cut out bright and colorful numbers you find in pictures and ads. Find a variety of numbers in different colors and sizes. Design and arrange the cutout numbers on a piece of construction paper, and glue them in place. One collage can include a random assortment of numbers, or it could have a theme, such as multiples of 4. You can also use the numbers as graphic elements to create figures and objects.

HOW MANY SQUARES?

197

Figure out how many squares there really are on a checkerboard!

What You'll Need: Checkerboard

This sounds easier than it is! You can easily see all the small squares on a checkerboard, but don't forget all the other squares that are made by combining the small ones! Don't just count the small squares—count every square! That means each small square counts as 1 square. Each group of 4 squares turns into a bigger square that is counted. Each group of 16 squares becomes another square that is counted. Count them all! Try this one day and then on another day—did you come up with the same number of squares each time? Keep trying!

PUZZLES FOR FIVE SQUARES

How many shapes can you make with five squares? Can you turn five squares into a box?

What You'll Need: Construction paper, ruler, pencil, scissors, tape

To try these puzzles, measure and cut out five 2×2-inch squares. Arrange the squares into a larger shape so all the squares are touching. The squares must be arranged so that squares with sides touching are lined up corner to corner. There are 12 different ways the 5 squares can be arranged. Find all 12 ways, and record them with pencil and paper by tracing the 12 different shapes onto construction paper. (Trace around the whole shape and also outline each square within the bigger shape.) Next, cut out the 12 different shapes. Eight of the shapes can be folded into boxes that can hold paper clips, buttons, or other small objects! Experiment to figure out which can be turned into boxes. Designate and mark the square that might be the bottom of the box. Then cut along the squares in order to fold and create square boxes.

LAYING THEM ON THE TABLE
Card games were probably invented in ancient China. Egyptian pharaohs also played cards, as did English kings and Spanish explorers.

WEIGHT OF WEALTH

199

Show me the money! Then show me how much it weighs!

What You'll Need: Counted coins, plastic bags, paper, pencil, grocery store scale

How much does a dollar weigh? Depends on the dollar, of course. Bundle up a dollar's worth of pennies in a sturdy plastic sandwich bag. Do the same for nickels, dimes, and quarters. Make a trip to your local grocery store, and weigh them on the fruit scale (ask permission first!). Jot down the weights in ounces. Now calculate how much $5.00 would weigh. How about $10.00 or $100.00?

200

PAPER CLIP MEASUREMENT AND ESTIMATION

Estimate and measure common objects with an uncommon measuring tool, a box of paper clips!

What You'll Need: Paper clips, pencil, paper

Take a look around your room, and make a list of several objects that are long, short, wide, and narrow. Guess how many paper clips long each object might be. How many paper clips long is a pencil? A shoe? What about your desk? Or your bedroom wall? Write down the name of each object and your estimation. Then measure! You can line paper clips up end to end next to the object to measure it, or you can connect the paper clips to make a measuring chain. Write the number measured next to your estimate. After you have measured all the objects on your list, compare your findings to your estimates. Did you estimate high? Low? Use your discoveries to make new estimates for different objects and test again.

WEIGH COOL

201

Are all things equal when it's time to measure the facts?

What You'll Need: Dowel, ruler, knife or scissors, string, 2 identical plastic dishes, measuring cup, sand, feathers, dry cereal, sugar, flour, paper, pencil

Make a simple measuring scale. Measure the dowel rod to find the exact middle. Ask an adult to carve a notch in the center of the rod with a knife or scissors. Tie a string around that center notch. Now hang the identical plastic dishes from each side of the dowel with string. Suspend the scale from a safe, still place such as a door frame or a ceiling hook. Now it's time to answer the question: Are all things equal? Do things that look the same or measure the same actually weigh the same? Not likely, but do this experiment to be sure. Measure ¼ cup sand, ¼ cup feathers, ¼ cup dry cereal, ¼ cup sugar, and ¼ cup flour. Examine the things you've measured, and decide if they look like they should weigh the same. Compare the substances using your handmade scale. Make notes about your discovery.

HOW DO YOU MEASURE THAT?

There are many things that are weighed and/or measured by scientists today. Some scientists measure the age of coral reefs, some measure the nutrients in cow's manure that will feed crops, and some measure how quickly the universe is expanding. Of course, all these scientists use different tools!

SIZING UP BODY PARTS

202

Measure and compare body-part length!

What You'll Need: Yarn, scissors, paper, pencil, tape

Measure and cut yarn pieces that are the same length as your hand, arm, foot, toe, head, and more. With the help of a friend or family member, also cut a strip of yarn that is as long as you are tall. Make a label for each piece of yarn and tape the body-part label to the piece of yarn. Then tape all the yarn strips on a wall next to one another and compare the varying lengths of the different parts of your body! For fun, arrange the yarn strips in order, from smallest to tallest.

THE PROBABILITY OF HEADS OR TAILS

203

Do a probability investigation.

What You'll Need: Coin, pencil, paper

What happens if a coin is flipped 100 times? Which will turn up more, heads or tails? Would the results be different with a different kind of coin? Test the probability of heads and tails turning up with 100 flips! Choose a coin and flip it 100 times, recording the result of each flip. Tally the results. Try the test again with a different kind of coin. Is the result the same or different? To simplify, test a penny, nickel, dime, and quarter, flipping each 20 times and recording the results of each flip. Compare the results.

THE GREEN STUFF

Want to turn your pennies into cool green cash? Line them up on a paper towel soaked in vinegar. It won't make them worth more, but it will turn them green (tops only, the bottoms will remain coppery brown).

TOOTHPICK SQUARES

Take the toothpick square challenge!

What You'll Need: Toothpicks, paper, pencil

Find the smallest number of toothpicks you can use to make a square. That's easy: 4. But what's the smallest number of toothpicks you can use to make 2 squares with a connecting side? Or 3 squares with connecting sides? What about 4 squares? Take the test! Make a chart with 2 columns. In the first column list the number of squares you are going to make with toothpicks (with connected sides). In the second column list the smallest number of toothpicks you can use to make those squares. Now make the toothpick squares, and record your findings on the chart. After constructing several toothpick squares, see if you can find a pattern in the numbers you recorded.

OLD-FASHIONED TEETH CLEANERS

People have been using toothpicks for thousands of years to clean their teeth—though dentists today prefer we use dental floss and toothbrushes! Toothpicks were found at the Ningal Temple in Ur, dating from 3500 B.C.

IT'S SO YUMMY

Explore the creative art of cooking! Preparing a recipe is more than just assembling ingredients. It's a scientific exploration and a creative art. When you try a new recipe, you learn how ingredients combine to make something new. Once you've tried a recipe, experiment by changing or adding ingredients. As a cook, you are a scientist at work, a food adventurer, and a creative artist. Plus, you get to make good things to eat! Note: Get adult permission before putting on your chef's hat, and ask for adult help with the cutting, cooking, and baking. Wash your hands before and after cooking, and wash all fruits and vegetables before eating or using in recipes.

PUMPKIN BUTTER

205

Make a delicious pumpkin butter in the fall, and use it on toast.

What You'll Need: 1 can pumpkin, 3 tablespoons honey, 1 teaspoon cinnamon, bowl, measuring spoons, pot, wooden spoon

Empty a can of pumpkin (not pumpkin pie filling) into a bowl. Measure and add the honey and cinnamon. Mix the ingredients together. Scoop the mixture into a cooking pot. (Have an adult help you with the cooking.) Cook over a low heat, stirring occasionally, until the mixture thickens (approximately 20 minutes). The pumpkin butter is ready to eat. Serve it hot on crackers, or refrigerate it in a jar and serve chilled with toast or muffins.

PERSONAL PIZZAS

206

Make your own pizza to order, and serve it up.

What You'll Need: English muffins; tomato sauce; cheese; olives, green pepper, mushrooms, or other pizza toppings; spoon; grater; aluminum foil

Use English muffins for your personal pizza base. With a spoon, spread tomato sauce on a muffin. Grate the cheese, and sprinkle it on top of the tomato sauce. Select toppings to place on the cheese. Use traditional toppings, such as olives, mushrooms, or green pepper slices, or come up with more unusual choices, such as raisins, dill pickle slices, or walnuts. Place your personal pizza on foil, and toast it in a toaster oven until the cheese melts and is bubbly.

HOMEMADE PRETZELS

207

Mix, mold, and bake pretzels in decorative and traditional designs.

What You'll Need: 1½ cups warm water, 1 envelope yeast, 1 tablespoon sugar, 1 egg, 4 cups flour, 1 teaspoon salt, cooking oil, measuring cups and spoons, 2 bowls, mixing spoon, cookie sheet, paper towel, pastry brush

Start by mixing the warm water, yeast, and sugar in a bowl and setting it aside. Beat the egg, and set it aside also. Get a cookie sheet ready for the pretzels by greasing it with a few drops of cooking oil. Spread the oil with a paper towel. Finish making the pretzel dough by adding the flour and salt to the yeast mixture. Stir all the ingredients together. With clean hands, break off pieces of the dough and form them into pretzel shapes. Roll the dough into a snake shape with your hands, and then twist it to make your pretzel designs. You can make any designs, such as letters or numbers—use your imagination! (The more you handle the dough, the thicker the pretzels will be when they bake.) Place the pretzels on the cookie sheet. Brush the top of the pretzels with the beaten egg so they will be shiny. Bake for 12 to 15 minutes at 350 degrees.

VERY BERRY SOUP

208

Make a fruit soup that's berry, berry good.

What You'll Need: 3 cups water; 1 cup apple, apple-berry, or berry juice; 1 cup blueberries; 1 cup blackberries; 1 cup strawberries; 1 cup raspberries; ¼ cup honey; 1 cinnamon stick; 1 lemon; plain yogurt or sour cream; measuring cups; mixing spoon; saucepan; blender

You can use equal parts of the blueberries, blackberries, strawberries, and raspberries, or you can alter the combination and ratio as you wish; just make sure you have 4 cups of berries. Have an adult help you with the cooking. To make the soup, combine the water, juice, berries, honey, and cinnamon stick in a saucepan. Bring the mixture to a boil and then cook over a medium heat for 5 minutes. Remove the soup from the heat, and let it cool. Take out the cinnamon stick, and discard it. Pour the soup in a blender, and add the juice of 1 lemon. Blend until the berry soup is smooth. Refrigerate. Serve chilled with a scoop of plain yogurt or sour cream on top. (Makes 4 to 6 servings.)

JUST THE BERRY FACTS

Blueberry plants can produce fruit for 40 to 50 years if the plants are well kept. The plants can also grow to be 20 feet tall!

PEANUT BUTTER

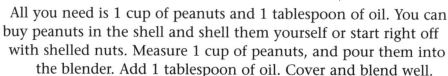

Blend some fresh peanuts, and turn them into yummy peanut butter!

What You'll Need: 1 cup peanuts, 1 tablespoon oil, measuring cup and spoon, blender, small jar, spatula, crackers, knife

All you need is 1 cup of peanuts and 1 tablespoon of oil. You can buy peanuts in the shell and shell them yourself or start right off with shelled nuts. Measure 1 cup of peanuts, and pour them into the blender. Add 1 tablespoon of oil. Cover and blend well. Use a spatula to scoop the peanut butter into the jar and refrigerate. But first, spread some on crackers and enjoy!

APPLE-BERRY JAM

Make a sweet and delicious jar of fruit jam with no sugar added.

What You'll Need: 2 green apples, 1½ cups frozen unsweetened strawberries, 6 ounces frozen unsweetened juice concentrate (apple, or white or red grape), apple peeler, knife, pot, wooden spoon, jar

This recipe will yield 1 jar of jam. Double the batch and give a jar as a gift! Peel, core, and slice 2 green apples. Put the apple slices into a cooking pot along with the unsweetened strawberries and the frozen juice concentrate (do not add water). Cook the fruit mixture over low heat for 40 minutes, stirring occasionally. (Ask an adult to help you with the cooking.) During the cooking time, the liquid will reduce and the jam will thicken. After 40 minutes, remove the jam from the heat and let it cool. When it has cooled, scoop it into a jar and refrigerate. If you liked this, try substituting frozen blackberries for strawberries!

STUFFED TOMATO SALAD

211

Put a nutty twist on cottage cheese with some sunflower seeds.

What You'll Need: ⅓ cup cottage cheese, 1 tablespoon sunflower seeds, tomato, sprouts, measuring cup and spoon, bowl, mixing spoon, knife

Mix cottage cheese with sunflower seeds in a bowl. Cut the top off of a tomato, and scoop out the seeds. Fill the tomato with the cottage cheese and sunflower seed mixture. Top with fresh sprouts. Serve for salad, snack, or lunch.

212

HUMMUS SPREAD

Serve this Middle Eastern delight as a dip for vegetables or pita bread slices, or as a sandwich spread.

What You'll Need: 1 garlic clove; 2 lemons; 1 can of chickpeas; 3 tablespoons tahini (available at a health food or grocery store); 1 tablespoon olive oil; 1 tablespoon apple cider vinegar; chopped vegetables, pita bread, or crackers; knife or garlic press; juicer; measuring spoon; bowl; fork

To make hummus, mince the garlic or mash it with a garlic press. Juice the lemons. Measure and mix all the ingredients together in a bowl. Mash with a fork to blend well. (For a smoother hummus, you can blend the ingredients in a blender.) Serve with chopped vegetables, pita bread, or crackers.

YOGURT CHEESE

213

Make cheese from yogurt to have for a snack with crackers.

What You'll Need: 1 container plain yogurt without gelatin, sieve, cheesecloth, bowl or jar, plastic wrap, crackers

Put 3 layers of cheesecloth in the sieve. Place the sieve so it sits suspended in a bowl or jar. Pour the yogurt on top of the cheesecloth. Cover the yogurt with plastic wrap, and put the whole thing in the refrigerator. Refrigerate for 2 days. During that time the liquid will drain out of the yogurt. The thick yogurt left behind is tangy yogurt cheese. After the 2 days, pour out the liquid in the jar. The cheese will be firm and ready to eat with crackers.

214

CHEESE BISCUITS

Create crunchy cheese cookies that can be sweetened with a spoonful of jam!

What You'll Need: Cooking oil, flour, 1½ cups grated cheddar cheese, 5 tablespoons margarine, cinnamon, cookie sheet, paper towels, measuring cups and spoons, bowl, grater, 2 butter knives or pastry cutter, fork, rolling pin, cookie cutters, butter or jam

Have an adult help you with the oven. With a paper towel and the cooking oil, lightly oil a cookie sheet. Sprinkle the cookie sheet with flour, and set it aside. Place the grated cheese into a bowl. Measure 1 cup flour, and add it to the cheese. Cut the margarine into small chunks with 2 knives or a pastry cutter, and add it to the bowl. Use a fork to mix the ingredients together into a smooth dough. Mold the dough into a ball, and place it on a flour-dusted surface. Use a rolling pin to roll out the dough to about ⅛ inch thick. Cut the cheese biscuits with cookie cutters, and place them on the prepared cookie sheet. Sprinkle with cinnamon. Bake for 10 minutes at 400 degrees. Eat plain or with butter or jam.

GUACAMOLE

215

Make this tasty south-of-the border treat medium or hot. Olé!

What You'll Need: Avocado, pinch of salt or dash of soy sauce, 1 tablespoon fresh lemon juice, chips, diced tomato (optional), scallion (optional), dash of powdered chili pepper (optional), knife, spoon, bowl, fork, measuring spoon

Guacamole is a simple and easy dip to make. Cut an avocado in half, and remove the pit. Scoop out the avocado pulp, put it in a bowl, and mash it with a fork. Add a pinch of salt (or a little soy sauce) and 1 tablespoon of lemon juice, and mix. That's all there is to it. The guacamole is ready for dipping with chips! Cover tightly and refrigerate if not serving immediately. (For more texture, add diced tomato to your guacamole. For a spicier guacamole, you can add a chopped scallion and a dash of powdered chili pepper to the mix.)

PLEASE STAY GREEN!

The reason avocado turns brown is that it contains an enzyme called polyphenyloxidase. The oxygen in air reacts with the enzyme and turns the avocado brown—this is the same enzyme that turns apples and potatoes brown. A little lemon or lime juice will prevent your guacamole from turning brown!

BANANA SHAKE

216

Whip up a simple fruity shake to share with a friend.

What You'll Need: 1 cup milk, ½ cup yogurt, ¼ cup frozen berries, 1 banana, blender, measuring cups

Measure and place the milk, yogurt, and berries into the blender. Peel a banana, break it into chunks, and drop it into the blender. Cover and blend well. Pour the fruit shake into cups, and toast to your health! (Makes 2 servings.)

CARROT SOUP

217

Cook a bright-colored, cheerful vegetable soup that's sweet and aromatic.

What You'll Need: 1 pound carrots, 4 cups water, 1 teaspoon salt, 1 teaspoon honey, ¼ cup cream, 1 tablespoon butter, pinch of nutmeg, ¼ cup chopped almonds (optional), knife, pot, blender, measuring cups and spoons

Have an adult help you with the cutting and the cooking. Wash and cut the carrots, and put them in a pot. Add the water and salt. Bring to a boil, then lower the heat. Cover the pot, and simmer the soup for 30 minutes. Then turn off the heat, and let the soup cool slightly. After cooling, pour the soup into a blender and add the honey, cream, butter, and nutmeg. Blend. Return the soup to the pot and heat before eating. Serve topped with chopped almonds! (Serves 4.)

218

ORANGE TAHINI POPS

Make a fruit ice-pop exotic with the addition of tahini (sesame spread).

What You'll Need: 4 oranges, 2 tablespoons tahini (available at a health food or grocery store), 1 teaspoon vanilla, pineapple juice and vanilla yogurt (optional), juicer, measuring spoons, blender, paper cups, craft sticks

Juice the oranges, and pour the juice into a blender. Add the tahini and the vanilla. Blend. Pour the juice mixture into paper cups and place in the freezer. Insert craft sticks when the mixture begins to thicken. When frozen, tear off the paper cup and enjoy the ice pop. (Makes 2 to 3 servings.) To make your pops fancier, fill the cups halfway with the tahini orange juice. Insert the craft stick when mixture begins to thicken. When almost completely frozen, add a second layer made from pineapple juice blended with vanilla yogurt. Freeze and eat.

NOW THAT'S A LOT OF JUICE!

The world's largest glass of orange juice was created by the Florida Department of Citrus. The glass is 8½ feet tall and is nearly 5 feet in circumference. It holds 730 gallons of Florida Valencia orange juice!

BAKED FRENCH FRIES

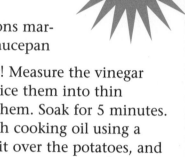

219

Cook up a batch of healthful fries—they are yum, yum, yummy!

What You'll Need: 1 tablespoon vinegar, water, 3 potatoes, cooking oil, 3 tablespoons margarine, salt, measuring spoon, large bowl, knife, paper towel, cookie sheet, small saucepan

These fries are baked in an oven instead of fried in deep fat—so much healthier! Measure the vinegar into a bowl, and add water to almost the top of the bowl. Peel the potatoes, and slice them into thin French fry strips. Drop the potatoes into the bowl of vinegar water after you slice them. Soak for 5 minutes. Remove the potatoes and pat dry with a paper towel. Lightly oil a cookie sheet with cooking oil using a paper towel. Put the potato strips on the cookie sheet. Melt the margarine, drizzle it over the potatoes, and toss them to coat evenly. Sprinkle them with salt. (You can also add paprika, onion powder, or other seasonings to give your potatoes zing.) Bake in the oven for 40 minutes at 375 degrees (have an adult help you with the oven). Remove and let cool before enjoying your French fry snack.

VEGETABLE DIP

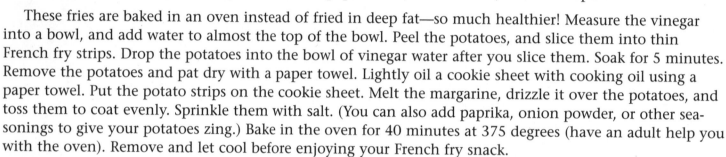

220

Mix together a zesty dip to snack on when your friends come over.

What You'll Need: Fresh vegetables, ½ cup cottage cheese, ½ cup plain yogurt, 1 package ranch dressing mix, knife, measuring cups, blender, spatula, plate

Wash and slice an assortment of fresh vegetables. Set the vegetables aside, and prepare the vegetable dip. Measure and place the cottage cheese and yogurt into a blender. Add the ranch dressing mix. Blend well. Use the spatula to scoop the dip onto individual plates. Serve the dip with the sliced vegetables.

CARROT RAISIN SALAD

221

Here is a fresh, cool salad that is good in spring, summer, fall, or winter.

What You'll Need: 2 carrots, 1 apple, ¼ cup raisins, ¼ cup walnuts, 1 teaspoon lemon juice, grater, bowl, measuring cup and spoon, knife

Grate the carrots and apple into a bowl. Measure and add the raisins. Chop the walnuts and add, along with the lemon juice. Mix. Enjoy! (If any of your guests are allergic to nuts, you can leave them out. This healthful salad is good with just the carrots, apples, and raisins!)

222

PIGS IN A BLANKET

Wrap up hot dog halves in a ready-to-go roll, and turn them into a "pigs in a blanket" party snack.

What You'll Need: 5 hot dogs, 1 tube ready-to-bake biscuit mix, milk, poppy or sesame seeds, knife, lightly greased cookie sheet, pastry brush, ketchup, mustard, pickle relish

Cut the hot dogs in half. Wrap 1 biscuit around each hot dog-half. Place the 10 wrapped hot dogs on a lightly greased cookie sheet. Dip the pastry brush in milk, and brush each of the biscuit blankets with a milk coating. Sprinkle with poppy or sesame seeds. (Have an adult help you with the oven.) Bake at 375 degrees for 12 minutes. Crusts should be golden brown. Serve with ketchup, mustard, and pickle relish.

TUNA BOATS

223

Turn a tuna salad into a sailing boat.

What You'll Need: 1 can tuna, ¼ cup chopped celery, 3 tablespoons mayonnaise, 1 tablespoon pickle relish, 2 tomatoes, 2 slices American cheese, can opener, spoon, bowl, knife, measuring cup and spoons, 4 toothpicks, fish-shaped crackers (optional)

Open a can of tuna, and drain the liquid out by squeezing the tuna with the can lid over a sink. Scoop the drained tuna into a bowl. Chop and add the celery. Measure and add the mayonnaise and pickle relish. Mix the ingredients together. Cut 2 tomatoes in half, and scoop out the seeds and tomato pulp. Spoon the tuna salad into the tomato shells. Place each filled tomato half on a plate. Cut the cheese slices diagonally to form 4 triangles. Insert a toothpick into 1 side of each triangle. Stick the end of the toothpick into the tuna salad in each tomato to create a cheese sail in a tuna boat. For an even more festive look, sprinkle fish-shaped crackers around each tuna boat. (Serves 4.)

HOW LONG HAVE WE BEEN EATING IT?

The ancient Sumerians ate cheese 4,000 years before the birth of Christ! But the many types and kinds of cheese that we know were probably developed by the monks who lived in the Middle Ages. During the Renaissance, many people stopped eating cheese because they thought it was unhealthy—now we know differently!

224

FROZEN BANANAS

Transform a banana into a cool treat for a hot day.

What You'll Need: 2 graham crackers, 3 tablespoons vanilla yogurt, 1 banana, waxed paper, rolling pin, bowl, spoon, knife, craft sticks, foil

Place 2 graham crackers between 2 sheets of waxed paper. Crumble the graham crackers by rolling a rolling pin over the waxed paper. Spoon the vanilla yogurt into a bowl. Peel a banana, and cut it in half. Insert a craft stick in each half. Dip the banana halves in the yogurt, and roll them in the graham cracker crumbs. Place the bananas on foil and freeze.

ZUCCHINI BREAD

225

Zucchini is not just a vegetable for dinner—it also can be used to make a sweet dessert bread!

What You'll Need: 2 eggs, 1 cup oil, 1 cup honey, 2½ cups grated zucchini, ¾ cup wheat germ, 2 cups flour, 1 teaspoon baking powder, 1 teaspoon baking soda, 1 teaspoon salt, 1 teaspoon cinnamon, 1 teaspoon ground ginger, 1 teaspoon ground cloves, 1 cup chopped nuts (optional), 2 loaf pans, cooking oil, paper towel, 2 mixing bowls, beater, sifter, measuring cups and spoons, spatula, toothpick

To bake zucchini bread, preheat oven to 325 degrees and grease 2 loaf pans. (Have an adult help you with the baking.) Using the beater, beat the eggs, oil, and honey together. Add the zucchini and wheat germ and stir. In another bowl, sift the flour, baking powder, baking soda, salt, cinnamon, ginger, and clove. Then add the dry ingredients to the zucchini mixture. Mix. Add the chopped nuts and mix again. Using the spatula, scoop the bread dough into the loaf pans. Bake for 1 hour. You can test to make sure the bread is ready by inserting a toothpick in the middle of a loaf and checking to see that the toothpick is clean when you remove it. Take the bread out the of oven and cool for 20 minutes in the loaf pans. Then remove the bread from the pan, slice it, and enjoy!

226

DEVILED EGGS

These eggs are devilishly delicious!

What You'll Need: 5 eggs, 3 tablespoons sour cream (or mayonnaise or ranch dressing), 1 tablespoon dry mustard, ¼ teaspoon salt, paprika, saucepan, knife, spoon, bowl, measuring spoons, fork

Make deviled eggs to serve or eat as an appetizer, snack, or accompaniment to lunch. First hard boil 5 eggs (have an adult help you with the stove). Put the eggs in a saucepan, cover with water, and bring to a boil. Reduce the heat, cover the pot, and continue to simmer for 15 minutes. Pour off the hot water, and run the eggs under cold water to cool them. Peel the shells, and cut the eggs in half lengthwise. Carefully scoop out the yolks, and put them into a bowl. Add the sour cream, mustard powder, and salt, and mash it all together with the egg yolks using a fork. Scoop the mixture back into the eggs. Sprinkle the eggs with paprika for garnish. Chill before serving.

TRICK OR EGG?

For many years, up to the present day, English children have gone pace-egging in the spring. The name comes from Pesach, the Hebrew Passover, which became Pasch, which means Easter. The children get dressed up in costumes with blackened or masked faces and go door-to-door, demanding pace eggs. Nowadays, they get candy or small coins instead of colored eggs!

TOASTY ZUCCHINI STICKS

227

These zucchini sticks make a crunchy, cheesy snack that's great for munching.

What You'll Need: 2 medium zucchini, ½ cup bread crumbs, ½ teaspoon salt, 1 tablespoon Parmesan cheese, 1 tablespoon sesame seeds, 1 egg, paprika, cooking oil, knife, 2 bowls, measuring cup, fork, cookie sheet, paper towel

Cut the zucchini into strips. In a bowl, measure and combine salt, bread crumbs, Parmesan cheese, and sesame seeds. In a separate bowl, beat an egg until it is frothy. Dip the zucchini strips into the egg and then into the dry mixture to coat. Place the coated strips on a cookie sheet that you have greased with cooking oil and a paper towel. (Have an adult help you with the oven.) Bake at 400 degrees for 15 to 20 minutes or until crispy and brown. Serve and munch.

228

APPLE CHEESE SALAD

Fruit and cheese are natural go-togethers.

What You'll Need: 1 apple, ¼ cup sliced Swiss cheese, ¼ cup diced cheddar cheese, ½ cup celery, 1 teaspoon lemon juice, ¼ cup mayonnaise, lettuce, bowl, knife, measuring cups, mixing spoon

Prepare a fruit-and-cheese salad for lunch, a snack, or as a side dish to a family meal. Have an adult help you core and dice the apple (you can use a red or a green apple). Cut the Swiss cheese into slices. Cut the cheddar cheese into chunks. Slice the celery. Put the apples, celery, and cheese into a bowl. Add lemon juice and mayonnaise. Mix and serve on lettuce leaves. (Makes 3 to 4 servings.)

SUNSHINE TEA

Prepare some tasty herbal tea by cooking it with sunshine!

What You'll Need: 1-quart glass or plastic jar with top, water, tea bags

Fill a clear jar with water. Add 3 tea bags of your favorite tea. Cover the jar, and set it outside in the sunshine on a warm sunny day. Let the tea brew for 4 hours. Remove the tea bags, and refrigerate until cool. Then treat yourself and your friends to a cool sun-brewed drink!

CHEESY CHIPS

Dress up your chips up with toasty cheese.

What You'll Need: 10-ounce bag tortilla chips, 1 cup grated cheese, ½ diced onion, ¼ diced green pepper, ¼ cup black olives, ½ cup sour cream (optional), ½ cup mashed avocado (optional), 1 diced tomato (optional), cookie sheet, measuring cups, knife, grater

Empty a bag of tortilla chips onto a cookie sheet. Sprinkle with grated cheese, diced onion, green pepper, and olives. Bake at 300 degrees for 8 minutes. Serve as is, or make your chips even fancier by topping with any (or all!) of the optional ingredients. (Serves 4 to 6.)

PITA CALZONE

231

It doesn't take much to make this cheesy Italian sandwich snack.

What You'll Need: 1 tablespoon red bell pepper, 3 tablespoons ricotta cheese, pita bread, knife, measuring spoon, mixing spoon, bowl, aluminum foil or paper towel

Finely chop a small slice of a red bell pepper. Mix the chopped red pepper and the ricotta cheese in a bowl, and scoop it into a pita pocket. Wrap the filled pita pocket in foil to bake it in the oven. (Have an adult help you with the cooking.) In an oven or toaster oven, bake it for 10 minutes at 375 degrees. You can also use the microwave: Wrap the filled pita pocket in a paper towel, and cook it for 45 seconds.

OATMEAL COOKIES

232

A chewy batch of homemade oatmeal cookies is sure to please friends and family alike!

What You'll Need: 1 cup margarine or butter, ¾ cup sugar, ¾ cup firmly packed brown sugar, 2 eggs, 1 teaspoon vanilla, 1½ cups flour, 1 teaspoon baking soda, 1 teaspoon salt, 1 teaspoon cinnamon, 3 cups oats, 1 cup raisins, measuring cups and spoons, 2 bowls, egg beater, sifter, wooden spoon, teaspoon, cookie sheet

Preheat the oven to 350 degrees (have an adult help you with the oven). Put the butter or margarine in a large mixing bowl along with the white and brown sugars. Beat until creamy. Then add the eggs and vanilla and mix well. In another bowl, sift the flour, baking soda, salt, and cinnamon together. Add to the egg mixture. Stir in the oats and raisins using the wooden spoon. Drop cookie dough onto the cookie sheet in little blobs using a teaspoon. Bake the cookies for 10 to 12 minutes.

233

BEAN SPROUTS

You don't have to go to a fancy restaurant to have fancy bean sprouts—grow your own!

What You'll Need: 3 tablespoons mung beans, measuring spoon, jar, water, cheese-cloth, rubber band

Measure 3 tablespoons of mung beans into a jar, and fill the jar with water. Place the jar uncovered in a dark cupboard, and let the beans soak in the water overnight. In the morning, cover the top of the jar with 1 layer of cheesecloth, and secure the cloth with a rubber band. Pour the water out through the cheesecloth. Add fresh water to the jar to rinse the beans, and then pour the water out again. Refill the jar with fresh water. Return the jar to the dark cupboard. For the next 3 to 4 days, rinse and pour off the water each morning and evening. Keep the sprout jar in the cupboard between rinsings. After 4 days, the sprouts will be ripe and ready to use in salads, to sauté in butter, or to add extra crunch in sandwiches.

THAT MAKES SPROUTING SENSE!

For more than 5,000 years, the Chinese have used sprouts for nutrition and even for medicine! Only recently, since World War II, Americans have realized how good sprouts are for us. Sprouts are a good source of vitamin C, protein (without the fat that comes with eating meat), and fiber.

GRANOLA

234

Make your own healthful breakfast cereal from a combination of fruits and grains.

What You'll Need: 3 cups rolled oats, ½ cup wheat germ, ½ cup shredded unsweetened coconut, ¼ cup sesame seeds, ¼ cup shelled sunflower seeds, ½ cup chopped nuts, 1 teaspoon cinnamon, ½ cup honey, ¼ cup salad oil, ½ cup raisins, 2 bowls, measuring cups and spoon, wooden spoon, cookie pan, freezer bag or jar

In a large bowl, mix the rolled oats, wheat germ, coconut, sesame seeds, sunflower seeds, chopped nuts, and cinnamon. Mix the honey and oil together in a separate bowl. Pour the honey and oil mixture over the dry ingredients. Stir everything (except the raisins!) together until well blended. Spread the mixture on a cookie sheet and bake at 325 degrees for 10 minutes. (Have an adult help you with the oven.) Add the raisins, and bake 5 more minutes. Remove the mix from the oven and allow to cool. Store in a freezer bag or tightly sealed jar. Serve with milk for breakfast.

235

CREAMY CELERY SPREAD

Plain celery becomes a fun treat!

What You'll Need: Celery sticks, ½ cup soft cream cheese, ⅓ cup chopped walnuts, ⅓ cup chopped olives, knife, bowl, measuring cups, fork

Wash and cut celery. Chop walnuts and olives. Measure the cream cheese, and put it into a bowl. Measure and add the chopped walnuts and chopped olives. Mix ingredients together with a fork. Spread the mixture on celery for a snack. This spread is also good on crackers or bread! (Note: You can buy a soft cream cheese that comes in a tub, or you can soften a package of cream cheese by taking it out of the refrigerator ½ hour ahead of time and then mixing it with 1 tablespoon of milk.)

DOUBLE-BAKED POTATO

236

Transform a simple baked potato into an unusual gourmet treat.

What You'll Need: 1 potato, ½ avocado, ¼ cup sour cream, ¼ cup grated cheese, knife, spoon, bowl, measuring cup, fork or potato masher

Bake a potato in a microwave oven. (Have an adult help you with the baking.) Allow the potato to cool. Then cut the potato in half, being careful not to tear the skin. Scoop the potato out of the skin and into a bowl. Add the avocado and sour cream. Mash the ingredients together well with a fork or potato masher. When thoroughly mixed, scoop the mixture back into the halves of the potato skin. Top with grated cheese. Return the potato to the microwave, heat up, and serve. (Makes 2 servings.)

237

TUNA MELT

Make an ordinary tuna sandwich into something a little fancier.

What You'll Need: 1 can tuna, ¼ cup chopped celery, 3 tablespoons mayonnaise, hamburger bun, cheese slice, can opener, bowl, knife, measuring cup and spoon, mixing spoon

Open and drain a can of tuna, and empty the tuna into a bowl. Chop the celery, and add it to the tuna along with the mayonnaise. Mix. Spread the tuna mixture on a hamburger bun. Place a slice of cheese on top. (Have an adult help you with the oven.) Cook in a broiler oven 3 to 5 minutes, until the cheese is melted. Serve and eat! (You can also make your tuna melt on an English muffin or a piece of bread if you prefer. To add more zip to your sandwich, include a slice of tomato under the cheese.)

HONEY LEMONADE

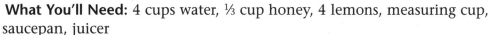

238

Make honey-sweetened lemonade ahead of time, and refrigerate it to have a refreshing drink ready on a hot day.

What You'll Need: 4 cups water, ⅓ cup honey, 4 lemons, measuring cup, saucepan, juicer

To make 1 quart of juice, measure water and honey into a saucepan. (Have an adult help you with the stove.) Boil for 2 minutes to dissolve the honey. Remove pan from heat. While the honey water is cooling, juice the lemons. Then add the lemon juice to the water, stir, and refrigerate it in a jar. (Fresh lemonade is also delicious hot, especially on a cold day! Or you can use the lemonade to sprinkle over a fruit salad.)

239

FROZEN FRUIT TREAT

Create a festive fruit treat to serve as a party dessert.

What You'll Need: 1 cup evaporated milk, 10-ounce package frozen unsweetened berries, 2 tablespoons honey, cupcake tin, foil cupcake liners, measuring cup and spoon, blender, craft sticks

Line two 6-cup cupcake tins with foil liners. Measure and pour evaporated milk, frozen berries, and honey into the blender. Blend until smooth. Pour the mixture into the cupcake foil liners. The treats will be about 1 inch thick. Place them in the freezer. When they start to harden, insert a craft stick in each. Freeze until hard. Serve them at your next party!

MEDIA MANIA

Working with words can be more than educational—it can be lots and lots of fun. Words are more powerful than magic—think about it! You talk to your friends and express amazing ideas with them, and you can even make someone feel happy by using complimentary words! So check it out. This section will tell you how to use wordplay to contact your favorite celebrities, make friends, try something new, speak your mind. Media mania is your writer's recipe for great new literary kicks!

WORD WONDER MAGNETS

240

Make headlines of your own that inspire and delight!

What You'll Need: Old magazines, scissors, cardboard, glue, magnet strips (available at craft stores)

Ever seen a word or a headline that inspired you? Hold on to that spirit with these terrific Word Wonder Magnets. Go through a stack of old magazines or newspapers until you see a word or headline that reminds you to do your best work, try a new sport, be a friend to someone who needs one, or do some other worthy activity. Cut out the word or words, and glue them to the cardboard. After the glue dries, cut away the excess cardboard and attach a small piece of magnet strip to the back. Hang up your headlines where they will remind you to always do your best!

BACKWARD & OPPOSITES

Woh tsaf nac uoy daer sdrow drawkcab? Can you sort out the ups and downs of ordinary words? These games will help you find out!

What You'll Need: 3×5 index cards, pens, pencils, clock or stopwatch

This brain puzzler sounds easier than it is. Write out 10 of your favorite words on 10 different 3×5 cards. Then write each word backward on the other side of the index card. Have your friend or a game partner do the same. Take turns showing each other the backward side of the cards. Keep track of how long it takes to solve each backward mystery. For an easier puzzler, consider opposites. Can you tell right from wrong? Black from white? Prove it. Write 25 words with obvious opposites on twenty-five 3×5 cards. On the back of each card, write the opposite of the word. See how long it takes to get a friend or partner to guess the exact opposite and say it out loud.

SECRET MESSAGES

In the late 1960s, the legendary rock group the Beatles played a backward game with their fans. They hid silly messages in their vinyl records—messages you could only hear by playing the record counterclockwise, or backward.

CREATIVE CROSSWORDS

242

Make up your own crossword puzzles, then share them with a friend!

What You'll Need: Paper, pens, pencils, ruler, graph paper

Add a new twist to an old favorite by making up crossword puzzles based on your favorite hobby, books, animals, or celebrities. Arrange your "down" and "across" words on the graph paper, writing 1 letter in each square. After you arrange the puzzle words, write your clues to match. Don't forget to number the words and clues. Hint: Don't make your word clues too difficult. Then copy the puzzle on a clean sheet of paper, and see how long it takes a friend to complete.

MAKING MONEY

243

Who and what would you honor if you could create paper money of your own?

What You'll Need: Paper, markers, real money to study, scissors

Real money reflects the culture of the land from which it originates. It tells you what is important to the people of that country. U.S. currency features American landmarks, leaders, and spiritual symbols. What would your money say about you if you had a land of your own? Why not design your own paper money and find out? Which heroes—both male and female—would you feature on the bills? Why? What landmarks best reflect who you are? Why? What color would your money be? Make your own money to find out more about yourself—so get out your art supplies and draw!

PICTURE PERFECT

244

Have fun putting pictures into words!

What You'll Need: Old magazines, paper, pens or pencils

Have you heard the old saying, "A picture is worth a thousand words?" Here's your chance to prove just how many words 1 picture can inspire. Go through a stack of old magazines and pull out pictures that appeal to you. It could be a dog running through a field. It could be a baby crying with a fever. It could be a grandmother opening gifts. Now see how many single words you can come up with to describe the picture. Take your time. This is a game you can play alone or with a friend. If you play with a friend, talk about the words you picked and why.

245

WHAT'S IN A WORD?

Pull words out of words with this fun puzzler.

What You'll Need: Dictionary, paper, pens or pencils, timer

Find a long and complicated word in your favorite dictionary. Write it out at the top of a blank sheet of paper. Now try to find words made up of the letters in the word you've selected—you can use the letters only as many times as they appear in the word. Give yourself 1 point for each word built from rearranging letters. Give yourself 2 points for words you find in the original word without switching the letters around. To add more of a challenge, put a 2-minute time limit on each round of your game.

WORD PICTURES

246

Paint a picture with powerful words!

What You'll Need: Blank paper, markers, crayons, colored pencils

Some words seem more powerful than their quiet cousins. "Big" seems small when compared to "enormous." "Wet" seems a little dry when held up next to "drenched." Pick your favorite powerful word, and carefully draw it in large block letters on a blank piece of paper. Then decorate the block letters with pictures and designs that help illustrate just what this blockbuster word means.

247

ANIMALRIFFIC

Is your favorite animal hiding in your favorite words?

What You'll Need: Pen, paper

Have you ever thought about how often your favorite animal is mentioned in another, often unrelated word? Take the ant, for instance. You find it in anticipation, antiperspirant, tyrant, and thousands of other words. Now pick your favorite animal (simple animal names such as "dog," "cat," "bug," etc. work best), and see what you can come up with. Illustrate your animalriffic words for an extra dose of fun.

ZOO FAVORITES
According to the experts at the Denver Zoo, most visitors consider the big cats and elephants their favorite zoo animals.

TO THE LETTER

248

Stick with one letter for storytelling fun.

What You'll Need: Paper, pens or pencils, colored markers or crayons

Just for fun, see if you can write a simple story using words that start with the same letter of the alphabet. Writing an "A" story? Start with, "An ant ate apples at Alaska's arctic area." See how long you can continue without breaking the letter chain. Don't get discouraged—this is sometimes difficult but always a blast! For extra fun, illustrate your story.

249

CALLIGRAPHY

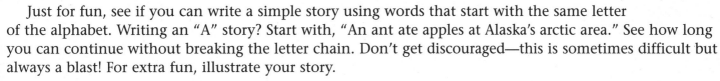

Thanks to calligraphy, how you write can be as expressive as what you write.

What You'll Need: An assortment of pens and papers

Have you tried exploring the fonts (type styles) on your home computer? Maybe you've seen an unusual letter style in your favorite book. Or maybe you've noticed surprising or interesting letter styles on book covers or in magazines. Each of these are examples of calligraphy—the art of lettering. Now's your chance to come up with a lettering style all your own. Try to develop letters, A to Z, that reflect your personal style. Ask your librarian to help you find books on calligraphy if you need inspiration.

WORD PICTURE BOOK

250

One picture is worth a thousand words—or is it the other way around?

What You'll Need: Dictionary, blank paper, crayons or markers

Thousands of new words are waiting for you to discover them in your favorite dictionary. So why not get started learning every single one? Open your dictionary to a page at random. Find a word you've never seen before. Read the definition carefully. Once you understand what the new word means, illustrate it on a piece of blank paper. Add a new page to your Word Picture Book each week.

251

BOOK PAGE BINGO

Search the pages of your favorite books to win!

What You'll Need: Books, bingo game, blank paper

Try something new with an old favorite. Pass out 1 bingo card and 5 books to each player. As the caller announces each letter/number combination (for example, B 12), players check to see if they have that square on their card. If they do, they must search through their books for the page number (page 12) and find a word that begins with that letter (B). The first person to raise their hand and show that combination, claims that bingo square and covers it on their card. The first person to cover a row—vertical, horizontal, or diagonal—on their card wins the game.

FRANKENSTEIN'S ANIMALS

252

Bits and pieces come together to make a new beast!

What You'll Need: Blank paper, markers, old magazines, glue, scissors

Do you love animals? Here's your chance to create a whole new species...or 2...or 3. Using animal body parts you find in magazine pictures, mix and match to make a whole new beast. Think a flying sea horse would be fun? How about a dog with 4 eyes? Or a turtle with fur! Anything is possible with a little imagination. Once your animal is captured on the page, write a short story about what makes it unique.

253

MYSTERIOUS SECRETS

Can you solve the mystery of the mystery? Check this activity to find out.

What You'll Need: Classic mysteries (such as Sherlock Holmes), notebook, pens

Mysteries are some of the most popular books sold in the United States and around the world. But what's the secret to a good mystery? The hidden treasure? The butler? The mysterious house guest? As you read your favorite mystery, take a few notes. Keep track of the secrets your fictional sleuth uncovers as he or she goes about solving the mystery. Then rewrite key scenes, changing those secrets. How would your changes affect the outcome of the story? Only you can decide!

GOOD SPORT

254

Complete this play to find out if sliding into home can have a whole new meaning.

What You'll Need: Paper, pen, dictionary

Do you love baseball? Live for football? Shoot for record-breaking hoops? Write out the special terms used in your favorite sport (words such as base, plate, and mound for baseball; dunk, court, and foul for basketball, etc). Now ask yourself...do these words have other meanings? Look the words up in a dictionary to see if they have other meanings. How would those meanings change your favorite sport? What would happen if Sammy Sosa slid into a home plate made of good china? Could John Elway score if all the receivers were parts of a telephone? Explore the magic of words and meanings—these would also make great pictures!

FAVORITE SPORTS
The top five sports in America are football, baseball, basketball, golf, and hockey (not necessarily in that order).

QUICK DRAW

Can you use words to describe an object without using the word that names the object?

What You'll Need: Magazines, glue, 3×5 index cards, box

Play this game with a partner. Find photos of simple objects such as dogs, cats, cereal boxes, and baseballs in an old magazine. Cut them out, and glue them on 3×5 cards. Put the cards in a box, and mix them up. Take a card from the box, and say words that describe the object without saying what the object is. See how long it takes your friend to guess what object you're trying to describe. Then it's your turn to guess!

MAGAZINE MATCH-UP

One person's trash is another person's great read!

What You'll Need: Magazines, wagon, paper bags

Once you've read a magazine cover to cover, is it time to throw it away? Not necessarily. Why not match old magazines with new readers? Gather up your old magazines. Ask your friendliest neighbors to do the same. Take an adult along, and go door to door with your wagon collecting magazines. Mix and match the pile into paper bags. Now make a few telephone calls. See if neighbors, senior citizen homes, or local hospital wards would like to participate in the drop-off. Even people in homeless shelters might like to catch up with the latest in magazines, and you can help!

257

NAME GAME

Who's who in the land of make believe?

What You'll Need: Old newspapers or magazines, scissors, blank paper, glue, markers, pencils or pens

Flip through an old newspaper or magazine and look for the names of famous or infamous people, such as Madonna, Butch Cassidy and the Sundance Kid, Elvis Presley, Michael Jordan, and Savage Garden, and cut out the names. Make a new name out of pieces of existing names—Savage Madonna, Elvis Jordan. Glue that name at the top of your blank piece of paper. Now make up a personality, a personal history, a whole new person to go with that made-up name. Maybe Elvis Jordan sings "Love Me Tender" as he makes jump shots!

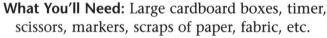

BOXING MATCH

258

How do you see things? Chances are, a lot differently than your friends might.

What You'll Need: Large cardboard boxes, timer, scissors, markers, scraps of paper, fabric, etc.

Playing with enormous boxes is always fun. So this activity is sure to be a knockout. Two teams each get a slip of paper with the same phrase written on it. The phrases will be instructions such as "Make your box a watery wonder," or "Make your box really fly." Without looking at the other team, you and your creative friends have exactly 15 minutes to decorate half the box to reflect that phrase. Do the decorations match? How did you interpret the phrase differently? Try another phrase on the other side of the box.

SPLITTING ENDS (AND BEGINNINGS AND MIDDLES)

What if "Once upon a time" could change with the turn of a page?

What You'll Need: Paper, scissors, pens or pencils, ruler

Are you a natural-born storyteller? Would you like to be? This crazy cut-up of a project can make it easy. Using a ruler, take 10 pieces of paper and divide each into 6 even sections. Write a very simple story, using 6 sentences, with a sentence in each section. Make the first sentence a "Once upon a time" character introduction, such as "Once upon a time, there was a green tree frog." The second describes where your character lived: "He lived in the wilds of a South American rain forest." The third sentence describes your character's special talent: "He was able to hop better than any animal in the realm." The fourth sentence describes the character's feelings: "But he was sad." The fifth tells why the character felt that way: "He was a very lonely frog." The last line tells how the character solved the problem: "So he found a friend in the pond." Write a story for each of the pieces of paper. Now cut the sections of each page so you can mix and match the lines of the stories. See what wacky combinations you can come up with.

RECYCLED GREETING CARDS

Bring old cards new life!

What You'll Need: Old greeting cards, clean colored paper, old magazines, scissors, glue, marker

Add new life to old cards with a little clean paper, some magazine scraps, and lots of imagination. Cover the inside of your favorite used cards with fresh paper or a collage of your favorite magazine photos. Write in a message that fits the occasion—you could even try writing a few short poems! Now you're all set to lift some spirits. Consider sharing your cards with lonely senior citizens or neighbors for an added bonus.

261 PICK-A-DAY BRIGHTENER

Pick a flower of encouragement that will bloom all year long.

What You'll Need: Pencil, paper, colored markers, scissors, paper plate, tape

Everyone could use an encouraging word from time to time. This basket of flowers will make it easy to pick a positive message when you need it most. Draw and cut out colorful paper blossoms about 3 inches wide. Write an inspirational quote or saying on the back of each flower. Ask your school librarian to suggest a book of good quotes to help you get started. But be sure to write some of your own quotes—you can come up with lots of good ideas. Fold a paper plate in half, and tape the sides together, leaving 4 or 5 inches at the top untaped. Decorate the folded plate to resemble a basket or flower pot. Slip your flowers into the paper basket, and draw from them whenever you need a lift.

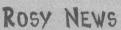

ROSY NEWS
Though thousands of kinds of roses have been grown for centuries, these five are among the current American favorites: Angel Face, Fragrant Cloud, Heritage, New Dawn, and Peace.

CHANNEL CHANGERS' WORD SEARCH

262

Channel surfing takes on alphabetical appeal!

What You'll Need: Paper, pencil, TV, remote control

On a blank piece of notebook paper, make a column listing each letter in the alphabet. Using the remote control, move from channel to channel, searching for words that begin with each letter. Play once, keeping track of how long it takes to complete your alphabetical search. Then play again to beat your own time. To make this a 2-player game, you and a friend can each go after words beginning with every other letter in the alphabet.

263

WORD SCRAMBLE

What will you say when you have to say it fast?

What You'll Need: Card stock, colorful markers, dictionary, timer, scissors, box

If you think you're good with words, this is the game for you. Write 20 of your favorite nouns (person, place, or thing words), 20 of your favorite verbs (action words), 20 of your favorite adverbs (words that modify verbs), 20 of your favorite adjectives (words that modify nouns), and a dozen each of "the," "a," "but," "or," "when," "why," "how," and "with." Cut each into 1-word strips, and toss them all into a box. Shake them up, dump them out, and see how many crazy sentences you can come up with in 2 minutes.

PLAY DAY

264

The play is the thing—and you can be the star.

What You'll Need: Spiral notebook, pen or pencil, imagination

If you've been bitten by the drama bug, you might want to put on your own performance. You can write, direct, and star in your own creative play. Make up 4 important or interesting characters. They could be rock stars or scientists, police detectives or circus clowns. What do they look like? Where are they from? Write it down. Now imagine what might happen to your characters. How did they meet? What do they do when they get in trouble? How do they get out of the fix? Write down everything you imagine they would say. Then get 3 of your friends to help you read the finished script.

265

REACH FOR THE STARS

Reach for the stars through the mail!

What You'll Need: Notebook paper, pen, envelope, stamp

Ever wished you could write to your favorite TV celebrity? What's stopping you? With a little research, you can tell the stars exactly what's on your mind. Write a short letter to the glamour queen or king of your choice (be careful with spelling and write neatly). Now comes the research. Grab your local newspaper television listings. What network makes your star's show? Match it up to the address below, and you'll know where to mail your message. In 4 to 6 weeks, you may even get a reply.

ABC: ABC, Inc., 77 W. 66th St., New York, NY 10023

FOX: Fox Family Channel, P.O. Box 900, Beverly Hills, CA 90213-2645

NBC: National Broadcasting Company, Inc., 30 Rockefeller Plaza, New York, NY 10112

UPN: United Paramount Network, 11800 Wilshire Blvd., Los Angeles, CA 90025

WB: The Warner Brothers Television Network, 4000 Warner Blvd., Bldg. #34R, Burbank, CA 91522

RHYME TIME

266

Time to find out if you're a true rhyming Simon.

What You'll Need: Notebook paper, stopwatch or egg timer, pens or pencils

Share this word game with a friend or play it solo. Look around the room and find a common object, such as a shoe. Take 30 seconds to write down as many words as you can think of that rhyme with that object (flu, zoo, boo, who, new, etc.). See who comes up with the most words. Or challenge yourself to beat your personal best.

PASS IT ON!

Writing a story is a team event when you pass it on!

What You'll Need: Old magazines, notebook paper, pens, pencils

Most writers work alone. But thanks to this activity, storytelling can be friendly fun. Go through a stack of old magazines and find a picture that really makes you think twice. Write a paragraph about the person, animal, place, or thing in the picture. Then pass the picture and your paragraph on to a friend. Ask them to add to the paragraph and pass it on to another friend. The next person adds a few sentences and passes it along, and so on, and so on, until you've built a whole story around the photo. Gather together and read the story aloud. Hint: You can play this game on the Internet via e-mail. Just find a picture on a Web site. Pass the Web address to your friends, along with your story. (Don't give out your name, address, or age to anyone you meet on the Web without your parents' permission!)

HEADLINE HUNT

268

Craft a crazy idea, using five words or less!

What You'll Need: Newspapers, scissors, paper, glue

Newspaper editors spend hours writing the perfect headlines. Now you can get a laugh out of their hard work. Clip all the headlines from an old newspaper, cut the words apart, and drop them in a box. Mix them up. Now try to make goofy headlines of the bits and pieces you've collected, and glue your favorite combinations on a page. Headline a crazy story only you could imagine—with a little help from the real news!

269

NEWSPAPER CAPER

Check out the who, what, when, where, why, and how of reporting the news!

What You'll Need: Newspapers, paper, pencil

Ever wondered what a real reporter does for a living? Why not do an interview of your own to find out? Thumb through a newspaper until you find an article that's interesting to you. Did the writer answer all your questions? Would you like to know more? Write down your questions and a short note of introduction. Send both to the reporter whose name is on the article, in care of the newspaper office. Don't forget to include a self-addressed stamped envelope and your e-mail address if you have one.

BLANKITY BLANKS

270

Even ordinary words can take on zany new meanings when you use them.

What You'll Need: Paper, pencils

Pick out a page from a story you've just read, or choose a poem you know. Write down a few of the key words from the story or poem. Now ask your friend or family member to replace those words on the page with words of their own, without reading the story first. Then insert their words in the real story or poem—the results will be rib-tickling surprises that really change the meaning of the story, 1 random word at a time!

271

PUZZLE POEMS

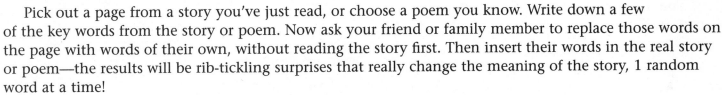

Puzzling over poetry? Try this activity on for size.

What You'll Need: Paper, markers, cardboard, glue, scissors, self-sealing plastic bag

Craving a puzzle with personal appeal? Write your favorite poem, classic or original, on a blank sheet of paper. Illustrate the poem with bright colors and drawings. Glue the paper to a piece of cardboard, and let it dry completely. Once it's dry, cut the stiff page into small pieces. You'll have your own personal puzzle poem to put back together and enjoy. Hint: Keep the pieces in a self-sealing plastic bag when you're not putting your puzzle together.

CYBER PALS

272

Find an electronic pen pal by surfing the Net!

What You'll Need: Computer with Internet access and Web browser

Pen pals are lots of fun, but it can be a real pain waiting for regular mail to deliver your next letter. Now you can conquer that time barrier, thanks to electronic mail. Use your favorite search engine (www.yahoo.com and www.excite.com are two good possibilities) to search for pen pal sites for kids. Follow the directions, and you could have an instant cyber friend by the very next day. This educational Web site (sponsored by Teacher Led Technology Challenge in Northern California) is a great place to start your cyber pen pal search: http://tltc.berkeley.k12.ca.us/penpals.html. (Be sure your parents give you approval before you do this activity. And never give out your real home address to anyone on the Internet!)

WELCOME TO THE INTERNET!

In 1988, statistics show that more than 62,000 people became new Internet users every week.

273 MATTER OF OPINION

What you think matters. It's time to speak your mind!

What You'll Need: Notebook paper, pen, envelope, stamp, newspaper

Has a news event ever made you mad? Has crime ever made you afraid? Has a sports hero ever made you proud? Why not tell your community how you feel? Write a letter to your local newspaper. Explain which current event made you think, and just what those thoughts were. End your opinion letter with your name, your age, and your phone number. Mail it to the editor of your local paper. Then watch the editorial page to see if your words make it into print.

FANTASY CREATURE 274

Build a body with scissors and glue!

What You'll Need: Old magazines, scissors, glue, paper, pen or pencil

Find out what it's like to be a mad scientist with this goofy cut-and-paste activity. Thumb through magazines until you find an interesting head, 2 unusual hands, a couple of dazzling eyes, some really amazing teeth, a wildly dressed body. Mix and match these body parts to create a fantasy creature sure to make you laugh. Glue your crazy creature to a piece of paper to show it off. Then write a funny story or poem about your crazy creature!

REBUS ROMP

Turn your favorite story into a rebus!

What You'll Need: Old magazines, scissors, paper, glue, favorite picture book

What is a rebus? It's a fun story in which key words—such as favorite characters or important settings—are replaced by illustrations. Maybe you wonder what your favorite classic would look like as a rebus story. Make a rebus version of a favorite story and find out. Cut key images in the story from old magazines or draw them yourself. Then write out the story, leaving spaces to glue the illustrations to your paper in the correct places. Glue on the illustrations, and share your finished rebus with a younger reader, your parents, or your friends.

COLOR OF COLOR

Why use red to describe your favorite flower when scarlet waits in the wings?

What You'll Need: Paper, pens or pencils

Professional writers know words have the power to paint pictures. Find out how great that power is with this colorful exercise. When you describe a red rose, is red really just red? Or is that vivid rose really scarlet? Is your blue sky just blue? Or is it a robin's egg blue horizon? Is the sun shining yellow, or is it bathing your world in gold? It's up to you. How many words can you come up with for the colors of the rainbow? Make a list to find out.

NOTE BY NOTE

Writing a tune is easy if you take it note by note.

What You'll Need: Piano or keyboard instrument

Writing tunes might seem like a difficult thing to do, but if you take it 1 note at a time, it can be done. Using a musical instrument with a wide range of notes and tones, pick a number between 1 and 10, and string that many notes together at random, keeping track of the pattern. If you pick 6, use 6 notes in the pattern. Now, using the same notes in a different order, create a new pattern. String the combinations together, and you have a tune of your own composition.

A YOUNG COMPOSER

The Finnish composer Jean Sibelius, 1885–1957, started playing the piano when he was five. He wrote his first composition, "Vesipisaroita" (Drops of Water), around 1895—he was only 10 or 11!

POETRY IN MOTION

278

Poetry is like painting pictures with words.

What You'll Need: Paper and pens

Think of sights you've seen that interested you or made you feel something. Maybe it was a bird flying, a dog chasing its tail, or a horse galloping across a field. Why not take a stab at writing a poem about it? Try to use powerful words—words that say more than you might think. For example, why use "big" to describe that Clydesdale horse when you could say "monumental"? Why say the dog was brown when you could say he was the color of chocolate? And remember, poetry doesn't have to rhyme to be good.

279

PICTURE PERFECT

Capture your life and loves in pictures, then share them with the world.

What You'll Need: Disposable camera, poster board, glue, markers, pen, index cards, photo album (optional)

Work around the house and neighborhood doing chores until you earn enough money to buy a disposable camera and to have the pictures developed. Then see if you can tell the story of who you are, using pictures alone. Are you messy? Take a picture of your room. Do you love animals? Take a picture of your favorite pooch. Take your time and really make every picture count. Mount them on poster board with glue, and write a few words under each picture describing why it means a lot to you. Or write your captions on index cards and arrange the cards and photos in a photo album.

BACK TALK

Can you talk backward? Nac uoy klat drawkcab?

What You'll Need: Paper, pens or pencils, tape recorder

Ever imagined what it would be like to say all your words backward? Why not give it a try? Write out a few sentences, carefully spelling each word backward. Practice reading the words aloud that way. Once you feel confident, record the backward phrases. Play them for your friends or parents to see if they can figure out the trick!

PET CAM

How does Rover see the world?

What You'll Need: Video camera or pen and paper

If you're old enough to use a video camera, this is a great way to understand your pets a little better. Get down on your hands and knees, grab your camcorder, and follow your dog or cat around the house. What do they see? What do they do? How do you think they might feel? Videotape "A Day With My Pet." (Be sure you use the video camera after getting your parents' approval!) If you don't have a video camera, make 4 or 5 illustrations of your own based on what you saw during your animal observations. Add captions; the results can be hilarious!

SENIOR INTERVIEW

282

We can shape the future if we learn about the past.

What You'll Need: Tape recorder, notepad, pen

Do you think all the good stories will spring out of the future? Think again. Interview a friendly senior citizen about what it was like growing up in the "old days." First, call to arrange a time for the interview. Prepare some questions in advance. You can ask, "How were things different when you were a kid?" "How much did gum cost?" "What did you do for fun?" "What was the scariest thing about life in your early years?" "What really made you laugh?" Record your interview with a tape recorder and take written notes. You can write a story about your interview, and then share your discovery with teachers, parents, and friends.

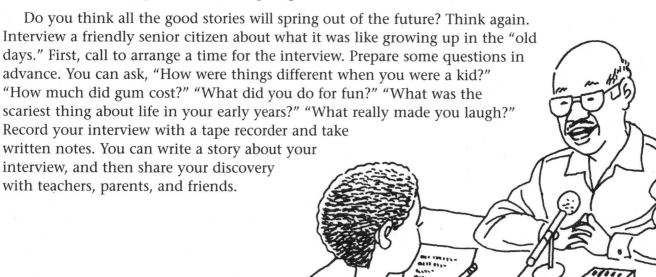

LONG LIFE

No one knows for sure which individual has lived the longest. But the *Guinness Book of Records* says Frenchwoman Jeanne Calment must have been among the top contenders. She passed away in August 1997, at the ripe old age of 122.

PAPER PROMISES

Cut out some favors the people you love can really use.

What You'll Need: Old magazines, scissors, paper, glue

Can't think of what to give Mom for her birthday? Dad for his special day? Grandma for Christmas? How about a promise on paper? Pledge to clean up your room, wash the dishes, or walk the dog—then put it in writing. Cut the letters you need to spell out the task from old magazines. Then watch their eyes light up when they discover their "gift."

INTERNET BINGO

284

Surfing the Internet can really spell F-U-N!

What You'll Need: Blank paper, computer with Internet connection and Web browser

You'll need adult permission for this activity. Internet bingo is like an electronic scavenger hunt. Spell out the word INTERNET on a sheet of notebook paper. Go to your favorite search engine (www.yahoo.com or www.excite.com are good possibilities), and type in whatever word comes to mind. It could be "dog" or "kite" or "video game." Spend the next hour searching for subject links that start with each letter in the word "Internet." E-mail a friend with the great new cyber stops you find along the way. (Remember, never give out your name, age, address, or e-mail address to any strangers you meet on the Net without your parents' permission.)

285

GEM OF A JOURNAL

When today becomes yesterday, your journal will tell the tale.

What You'll Need: Journal, pen or pencil

For generations, diaries and journals have not only helped writers understand their world, it has also given readers in later times a chance to know what life was like in the past. Consider keeping a daily or weekly journal of your thoughts about your life. Talk about what you like to do, to eat, to see, to enjoy. Put in details likely to change in coming years, including what things cost, political leaders, and popular styles of clothing. Years later, you'll find it interesting to read through your old journal. And, who knows? Maybe future generations will be grateful to you for recording your impressions of today.

HISTORIC JOURNAL

One of the most famous journals ever written was the *Diary of Anne Frank*. It told the story of a young Jewish girl's struggle to survive during World War II.

SCIENTIFIC SLEUTHING

Scientists probe the questions of how things work and why things act the way they do. But science is not just for scientists. Everyone is interested in the world around them and what makes things tick. You can learn a great deal about your world by observing and performing experiments right in your own backyard or kitchen. Here are some activities to get you started investigating at home!

KALEIDOSCOPIC VIEW

286

Make your own kaleidoscope, and view fantastic symmetrical patterns.

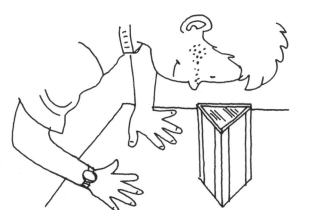

What You'll Need: 3 rectangular mirrors; masking tape; cardboard; pencil; scissors; small pieces of colored paper, buttons, glitter, or other small, colorful objects

To make the kaleidoscope, tape 3 mirrors together, with the reflective sides facing in, to create a triangular shape. Set 1 of the open ends of the triangle on a piece of cardboard and trace it. Cut out the cardboard triangle, and tape it over 1 open end of the mirror triangle. Set the mirror triangle on its cardboard bottom end. Drop pieces of small colored paper, glitter, buttons, and other small objects inside. Then peek inside to see the colored patterns created and reflected in the mirrors. Gently shake the kaleidoscope to make new patterns!

DISCOVER HIDDEN LEAF COLORS

Preview fall colors in a spring or summer leaf.

What You'll Need: Green leaves, plastic bowl, sand, rubbing alcohol, rock, glass jar, paper, paper clips

The reds and yellows and oranges seen in fall leaves are always there, but they are hidden during the year by the greater amounts of green pigment in the leaf. You can perform an experiment to separate the colors in a leaf so you can see some of the hidden colors.

Gather some green leaves. Put a few tablespoons of sand in a plastic bowl and add the leaves. With adult supervision, add enough rubbing alcohol to cover the leaves. Crush them into little pieces using a rock. (Be sure to wash your hands after touching the rubbing alcohol, and keep alcohol away from younger children in the house.) Crushing the leaves in the rubbing alcohol will pull the pigment out of the leaf and turn the alcohol green. Carefully pour the green alcohol out of the bowl and into a glass jar. (Discard the sand.) Now, roll a piece of paper into a cylinder and clip the ends together with a paper clip. Place the paper cylinder in the jar of alcohol, and leave it overnight (keep it away from any flame). The leaf pigments will creep up the paper. The pigments climb at different speeds, causing the different colors to separate from each other. In the morning, when you check the paper, you will be able to see the colors that were hidden in the leaf on the paper cylinder.

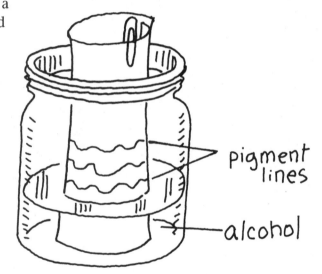

pigment lines

alcohol

RAIN GAUGE

288

Measure, record, and chart daily, weekly, or monthly rainfall.

What You'll Need: Jar, ruler, permanent marker, chart paper, pencil

Compare your measurements to those recorded in the newspaper! Use a cylinder-shaped jar or a square container with straight sides for your gauge. (You can also use several containers of different sizes to test if the results will be the same in different places in your yard.) Measure and mark inch and half-inch marks on the side of the jar or container, measuring from the bottom up. Place the gauge outside in an open area. Check the rainfall in each 24-hour period. You can use separate gauges for daily, weekly, and monthly recordings. Empty the daily gauge after each recording, and set it back outside to measure the next day's rainfall. Chart your results.

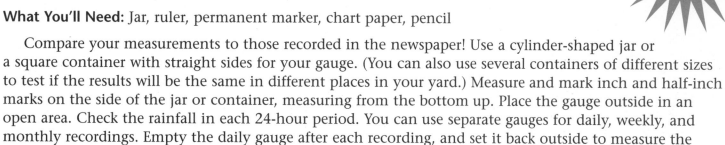

289

SECRET MESSAGE MAKING

Write an invisible message, and then amaze your friends by making it appear.

What You'll Need: Lemon juice, grapefruit juice, milk, or baking powder; paper; paintbrush or cotton swab; scrap paper; iron

Invisible messages can be written using several different kinds of substances. You can experiment with different "secret inks." Try writing messages with lemon juice, grapefruit juice, milk, or baking powder. Write your message on a piece of paper using a paintbrush or a cotton swab. Write carefully because you won't be able to see the message while you're writing it! To make the message appear, have an adult help you place the message paper between 2 sheets of scrap paper on an ironing board, and then iron the papers with a warm iron. Your message will appear as if by magic—but it is really a chemical reaction that happens quickly because of the heat of the iron.

HOW MUCH RAIN IN A RAIN FOREST?

A rain forest gets between 60 and 100 inches of rain every year—some have even gotten as much as 400 inches in a year!

PERISCOPE

290

Turn an empty waxed paper box into a spy tool for looking around corners, over walls, and out of windows.

What You'll Need: Empty waxed paper box, scissors, masking tape, 2 small mirrors (about 2×3 inches)

Ask an adult to cut off the cutting edge of the box. Tape the box closed with masking tape. Cut out a small square on the top end of 1 side of the box. Cut another small square out at the bottom end of the opposite side of the box. On a third side (a side between the 2 sides with the cutout holes) cut a diagonal slit at each end of the box. Cut each slit so that the bottom of the slit is level with the bottom edge of 1 of the cutout squares, and the top of the slit is level with the top edge of the cutout square. The bottom slit's bottom should be close to the cutout hole and slant away from the hole. The top slit should slant in the same direction as the bottom one. Cut identical slits on the opposite side of the box. Each slit should be a little bit wider than the mirror width so the mirrors will fit in the slits. Slide a mirror into each slit. If the mirrors are 1-sided, slide them in so the reflective sides face the holes. Secure the mirrors in place with tape. Hold the periscope upright, and look into the hole at the bottom. You'll see what's caught in the reflection from the top hole!

Up Periscope!

A submarine has two periscopes: an attack periscope and a search periscope. The search periscope is used to look for targets and also for guidance as the sub navigates through the water. The attack periscope is smaller than the search periscope and is used if a sub is ready to attack—hence its name.

DIRT DISCOVERY

291

There's more to dirt than you think! Find out what it's made of.

What You'll Need: Waterproof table covering, jar with lid, spoon, dirt, pitcher of water, paper towels, magnifying glass

Cover your work surface. Fill a jar halfway with dirt. Add water nearly to the top of the jar. Put the lid on, and tighten it securely. Shake the jar vigorously for a half a minute, and then set it down. Let the jar stand until the dirt and water settle. The soil will settle into layers. Observe the layers in the jar, and see what you can tell about them. How many layers are there? Which layer is made of the biggest particles? Which is made of the smallest? Can you guess why? To further examine the different layers and what they are made of, you can sort out the soil materials and examine them. Use a spoon to skim off the objects floating in the water. Place them on a paper towel. Then carefully pour off the water on the top and scoop out the grains of the next level onto another paper towel. Do the same if there is another level. After each layer has been placed onto towels, they can be examined with the magnifying glass. What else can you tell about the different layers after further examination? You can also do this experiment with dirt you have collected from different areas and compare your findings. Draw pictures of each jar full of soil after you have shaken it and the dirt has settled to make picture comparisons.

SPIN A COLOR WHEEL WHITE

292

Spin a color wheel, and watch it turn white!

What You'll Need: White tagboard or paper plate, protractor, pencil, paint, paintbrush

Cut a circle out of white tagboard (or use a white paper plate). Using the protractor, measure and mark 7 even, pie-shaped sections on the circle. Paint each section with 1 of the 7 colors of the rainbow. The colors must be in the order in which they appear in the rainbow (violet, indigo, blue, green, yellow, orange, red). When the wheel is dry, punch a pencil through the middle to make a spinner. Spin the wheel, and watch what happens. If you spin the wheel fast enough, the 7 colors blend and appear as white.

PERSONAL SHADOW CLOCK

Create a personal shadow clock, and tell time with your own shadow!

What You'll Need: Chalk, rocks, or sticks; watch; permanent marker

Find a sunny spot outside to make the clock. Choose a place for the center of your clock. If you are making your clock on a patio or concrete area, mark the center with chalk. If your clock will be on a lawn or dirt area, use a rock or insert a stick in the ground to mark the center. To make the hour markings, go outside every hour, on the hour, and stand on the center of your clock. Then make a mark on the ground where the tip of your shadow hits. (Have a friend or family member help you!) You can make the hour markings in the same way you marked the center, using a rock, chalk, or a stick inserted in the ground. But this time, you'll need to label the time, too! Write the hour number on concrete with chalk or use a permanent marker to write the hour on a rock or stick. After the clock is made, you can return to it at any time on another day, stand in the center, and determine the time of day by noting where the tip of your shadow lands.

THE U.S. TIMEKEEPER

The U.S. Naval Observatory, in Washington, DC, is the official source of time for the Department of Defense and is the official timekeeper for the United States.

WATER SCALE

294

Measure an object's volume using water.

What You'll Need: Large bowl, baking pan, water, assorted items (apple, rock, etc.), clear measuring cup

Place a large bowl in a baking pan, and fill the bowl to the rim with water. Gently drop an apple, a rock, or another item inside the bowl. The water will overflow into the baking pan to make room for the object dropped into it. Now, carefully remove the bowl from the pan and pour the displaced water into a clear measuring cup. Use the information to compare the volume of different objects.

295

CAPTURING LEAF VAPOR

Do leaves actually "breathe"? Check it out!

What You'll Need: Plastic sandwich bag, twist tie, small pebble, measuring spoon

Capture and measure how much water vapor a leaf releases into the air in a week's time. Trees drink water through their roots, and send it up to all parts of the tree. Leaves use the water they need and "breathe" out the excess in the form of water vapor. You can catch and measure the vapor using a plastic bag. On a warm, sunny summer day, put a pebble in a plastic bag and place the plastic bag over a tree leaf that gets a lot of sun. Secure the bag over the leaf with a twist tie. After a few hours, return to observe the leaf. You will begin to see moisture collecting inside the bag. Leave the bag on the leaf for 1 week. After a week, take it off and carefully measure the water collected with a measuring spoon. This will tell you how much water vapor your leaf has produced in a week's time. (A small leaf will produce approximately ¼ teaspoon of water in a sunny week.)

LOOK-ALIKE TESTING

296

Salt and sugar look alike, but how, besides taste, are they different?

What You'll Need: Table covering, smocks, salt, frying pan, measuring cups and spoons, sugar, clear plastic cups, water, food coloring, ice cube tray

You can perform several tests to find out how the molecules in these 2 look-alike substances act differently under different conditions. With adult supervision, you can perform a melting test. On your own you can do a dissolving test and a freezing test. Be sure to cover your work surface when doing your experiments.

Melting Test (ask an adult to help you): Place ½ teaspoon of salt on 1 side of a frying pan and ½ teaspoon of sugar on the other side. Tap down each pile so it is flattened. Heat the pan slowly for 3 minutes. Then remove the pan from the heat. Watch and see what happens to the different piles.

Dissolving Test: Fill 2 glasses with ½ cup of water each. Add 2 teaspoons of salt to one glass and 2 teaspoons of sugar to the other glass. Add a different color of food coloring (1 drop) to each glass to distinguish the solutions from each other. Let the solutions stand for an hour, and then check for crystal formations. Crystals will form differently in each solution.

Freezing Test: Fill 2 glasses with ½ cup of water each. Add 2 teaspoons of salt to the first and 2 teaspoons of sugar to the other. Color each solution a different color with a drop of food coloring. Pour 1 solution into the cups at one end of an ice cube tray and the other solution into the cups at the other end. Place the tray in the freezer for 2 hours. Then check to see if there is a difference between how the substances reacted to the cold.

REVERSE GARDEN

297

Plant a garden in reverse, and investigate what "biodegradable" means.

What You'll Need: Deep pan, trowel, soil, variety of garbage (apple core, dried leaves, newspaper, plastic foam, old sock, empty can), watering can or pitcher

Instead of planting seeds and bulbs and watching plants and flowers sprout blossoms, bury different kinds of garbage and observe them as they decompose. Fill a deep pan with soil, and bury several kinds of garbage under the soil. Plant an apple core, some dried leaves, a crumpled piece of newspaper, a piece of plastic foam, an old sock, and an empty can. Water your garden every couple of days. Dig up the garden after a week, and see what is happening to the items. Rebury your decomposing plantings, and continue to water every couple days. Dig up the garden again, and observe it after 2 or 3 more weeks. Then replant it one more time, and check it in several more weeks. Note what changes and how and what does not. You may want to keep a journal and make sketches each time you unearth your garden for observation. (Be sure to wash your hands or wear disposable gloves each time you work in your reverse garden.)

298

FOSSIL IMPRINTS

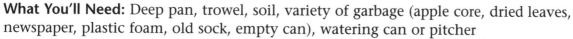

Learn about fossils by making a few of your own.

What You'll Need: 2 cups flour, ½ cup salt, ¾ cup water, bowl, measuring cup, objects for fossil making (leaves, shells, twigs, or boiled and washed chicken leg bones), rack

Measure and mix together the flour, salt, and water to make a salt dough. Knead the dough for 5 minutes, and form it into small balls. Flatten the balls to prepare them for a fossil print. Make impressions in the dough with different objects. Make 1 print in each flattened ball. Place the fossils on a rack, and let them dry for several days.

CREATE CRYSTAL CREATURES

299

pencil

sugar water

pipe cleaner

Dip decorations and paper sculptures in a crystal solution, and watch your work crystallize overnight!

What You'll Need: Waterproof table covering, water, saucepan, sugar, plastic cups, chenille stems, string, scissors, pencils, food coloring, index cards, Epsom salts, alum, permanent markers, pie pan

Cover your work surface. Have an adult help you throughout this activity. Heat a cup of water until it begins to steam. Remove it from heat and stir in 2 cups of sugar. Then pour the solution into plastic cups. Mold chenille stems into decorative shapes (star, heart, cat, initials). Tie one end of a piece of string to a chenille stem shape and the other end around a pencil.

Let the shape sit in the solution by balancing the pencil on the rim of the cup. Leave it overnight, and then remove it from the solution and let dry on a paper towel. When dry, the decorations will be covered with shiny crystals. They can be hung in a window, from a shelf, or anywhere! For larger crystals, allow the chenille stem to soak for a longer time in the solution. For colorful crystals, add food coloring to the crystal solution.

Create crystals of a different texture by using different materials. Follow the same recipe, replacing the sugar with Epsom salts (wash your hands after touching Epsom salts). Or try adding alum (available at the drugstore) to hot water for a different crystal solution: Ask an adult to heat a cup of water until it steams, pour it into a cup, and stir in alum spoonful by spoonful until no more will dissolve. Then suspend the chenille stem shape in the solution. To make a crystal sculpture, fold an index card in half. Draw an animal, person, creature, or shape on the card using the edges of the card as the bottom. Cut out the shape. Pour one of the crystal solutions into a pie pan. Stand the paper shape in the solution, leave it for several days, and watch the crystals grow to cover it!

KITCHEN GARDEN

300

Grow a garden from foods you find in your kitchen!

What You'll Need: Sweet potato, toothpicks, jars of water, avocado, pot, potting soil, onion or garlic, shallow bowl of water, apple seeds, paper towel, plastic bag

To grow a sweet potato plant, poke 3 or 4 toothpicks into the middle of the sweet potato. Set the potato in a jar of water so the toothpicks rest on the jar rim (half of the potato should be under water). Set the jar in a sunny place, and watch vines begin to grow. For an avocado plant, remove the seed from an avocado and rinse it. Insert 3 toothpicks around the middle of the pit, halfway between the top and the bottom. Place the pit in a jar of water with the pointy side up. Set the jar in a sunny place, and make sure the water level doesn't fall below the pit. After the pit has produced both a root in the water and a shoot above, you can plant it in potting soil. Plant the pit so that ⅔ is below the soil and ⅓ is above. Water the growing avocado tree, and keep it in a sunny spot. To sprout an onion or garlic plant, cut an onion or garlic clove in half, and set one of the halves in a bowl of water. Soon a shoot will sprout up. To grow apple seeds, you will have to convince them they've been through the winter. Wrap apple seeds in a wet paper towel, and keep them inside a plastic bag in the refrigerator for 6 weeks. Take them out and plant them in soil. Put them in a sunny spot, keep them moist, and soon apple trees will begin to grow.

BUG HOUSE

301

Make a simple bug home, and capture an insect to observe for a day or two.

What You'll Need: Clear plastic cup, plastic spoon, dirt, twigs, leaves, rock, water, bottom of a leg of a nylon stocking, twist tie

Scoop a few spoonfuls of dirt into a plastic cup. Add some leaves and twigs and a rock. Moisten the soil and leaves with few drops of water. Set the cup inside the end of the nylon stocking. Now find an interesting bug. Place the bug inside the cup. Seal the top of the stocking with a twist tie. Observe your insect guest for a day or 2, and then set it free outside again.

COMPARATIVE PARACHUTING

Make parachutes from different materials, and observe how air pressure helps them float!

What You'll Need: Paper grocery bag, scissors, string, tape, washer

To make a paper-bag parachute, cut a large square out of one side of a paper grocery bag. Cut the corners off the square to make it into an 8-sided shape. Cut 4 long pieces of string, and fold them in half. Tape the ends of each piece to 1 of the 4 original square sides to form a loop. Tie the loop ends of the 4 strings together, and then tie them to a washer. For a fabric parachute, cut 4 pieces of string and tie 1 to each corner of a handkerchief. Tie the ends of the strings to a washer or weight. You can also experiment with making parachutes out of other materials and comparing the results. Make parachutes from plastic garbage bags, paper towels, or burlap fabric. Experiment using different weights, such as nuts, bolts, clothespins, and pieces of wood. Drop your parachutes from different heights, and watch them float. Try dropping a parachute from the top of the staircase to see what happens. Try folding up a cloth parachute and throwing it up in the air to see if it floats down. Compare your results with different materials, weights, and heights.

THAT'S FAST!

When sky divers jump from a plane, they are going the same speed of the plane, between 90 to 110 mph (miles per hour), but they are traveling horizontally. Within the first 10 seconds, though, the sky divers accelerate to 115 to 130 mph, going straight down. Experienced sky divers can reach speeds over 160 to 180 mph!

BARK CASTING

303

Record and compare the bark patterns of different trees.

What You'll Need: Modeling clay, rolling pin, self-hardening clay

To make a tree bark impression, roll out a piece of modeling clay into a flat sheet. Press the clay onto a tree trunk hard enough for the bark to create an impression in the clay. Then carefully peel the clay off the tree, keeping the molded texture intact. To make a permanent cast of the tree bark, roll out a piece of self-hardening clay. Flatten it into a sheet the same size as the modeling clay impression you made. Place it on top of the modeling clay, and gently press it onto the ridges so that it captures all the textures but does not erase them. Gently lift off the clay and let dry for 2 or 3 days. Do this for several types of trees, and compare the different textures.

304

LIQUID DENSITY TEST

Do all objects of the same size have the same density? Find out!

What You'll Need: Clear plastic cup or glass jar, corn syrup, salad oil, water, small objects (paper clips, buttons, macaroni, etc.)

Use the density of liquids to test the density of small objects. Fill a clear cup or jar a third full with corn syrup. Fill the next third of the jar with salad oil. Then add water to fill the top third. Drop small objects into the jar and observe on what level they stop and float. Objects will float at different levels depending upon their density in relation to the density of the different liquids. If the density of an object is greater than a liquid's density, it will sink through that liquid. If an object's density is less than a liquid's density, it will float on that liquid. After experimenting a little, choose some new objects to test and try predicting the level on which they will float or sink before dropping them into the jar!

WATER ON THE MOVE

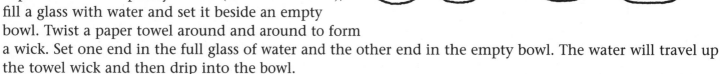

305

Explore the capillary action of water, that is, how water moves through the tiny spaces in fiber.

What You'll Need: Celery, glasses, water, food coloring, scissors, white carnation, string, small bowls, paper towel

To watch water move through plant material, stand a stalk of celery in a glass of water that has been colored with food coloring (see illustration 1). You will be able to see the water traveling up the celery as the celery stalk changes color. If you can get a white carnation, you can create a more dramatic demonstration (see illustration 2). Snip the stem of the white carnation to divide it in 2. Set each stem section in a separate glass of water that has been colored with a different color of food coloring. The colored water will travel up the halves of the carnation stem and mix at the top in the flower.

To watch water make its way through a piece of string (see illustration 3), fill 4 bowls with water and add a different color of food coloring to each bowl. Cut a piece of string and dip the end of the string into 1 bowl. Then drape the string over the edge of the bowl and over the next bowl so that it dips slightly into the water in that bowl. Continue until the string touches the water in each bowl. Soon you will observe the colored water creeping along the string out of the bowls.

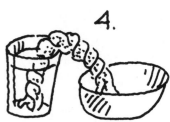

For another experiment to give you more experience with capillary action (see illustration 4), fill a glass with water and set it beside an empty bowl. Twist a paper towel around and around to form a wick. Set one end in the full glass of water and the other end in the empty bowl. The water will travel up the towel wick and then drip into the bowl.

REFLECTIVE EXPERIMENTING

Mirrors and light are fascinating—reflect on it and experiment!

What You'll Need: Cardboard, comb, tape, flashlight, paper, pencil, mirror, 2 small rectangular mirrors, small object

Perform several experiments to explore mirrors and the reflections they can produce.

Experiment 1: In a piece of cardboard, cut a 1-inch hole. Tape a comb over the hole. In a darkened room, hold the cardboard upright and set the flashlight behind it so it shines through the hole. Hold a mirror in front of the hole to capture the reflection. Turn the mirror to investigate how it reflects light at exactly the same angle it hits the mirror.

Experiment 2: Write something backward on a piece of paper. Hold the paper in front of a mirror; your backward message will read forward in the mirror!

Experiment 3: Tape 2 small mirrors together on one side to form a right angle. Sit the mirrors on their sides and place a small object between them. You will be able to see many sides of the object in the mirrors. Move the mirrors closer together and farther apart and observe what happens to the images. You can also try placing the mirrors (untaped) facing each other with the object between them in order to see an endless reflection.

CLAY BOATS

307

Mold and model clay to find what shape floats best.

What You'll Need: Bucket or large bowl; water; plastic table covering; modeling clay; paper clips, pennies, or marbles

Fill a bucket (or even a large bowl) with water. If you are working inside the house, cover the table with a plastic table covering. Then take a lump of modeling clay, and experiment! Try shaping the clay into different kinds of boats until you find a shape that will float successfully. Once you have figured out what kind of clay shape will float in water, experiment further by testing how many pennies, paper clips, or marbles your boat can carry without sinking. Make an estimate before testing. Then keep adding a penny or paper clip until you've sunk your boat!

308

MAGNET MAKING

Magnetize an ordinary nail by rubbing it with a magnet.

What You'll Need: Steel nail, paper clip, magnet

Try picking up a paper clip with an iron or steel nail. What happens? Now rub the nail with a magnet 50 to 100 times, always rubbing in the same direction. Try picking up the paper clip again. The atoms in the nail lined up in the same direction when you rubbed it with the magnet. This causes the nail to become magnetized, which means it will act like a magnet. Test your new magnet, and see what small objects it attracts. If you rub it more does it become stronger? You can also magnetize a paper clip and test the comparative strength of the 2 magnets you have made.

TWIG COLLECTING

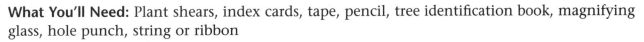

309

Make a collection of twigs gathered from trees in winter.

What You'll Need: Plant shears, index cards, tape, pencil, tree identification book, magnifying glass, hole punch, string or ribbon

The twigs of each kind of tree have unique shapes and characteristics. You can collect an assortment of winter tree twigs, note the variety of characteristics, and compare and sort them. If you have a good twig or tree identification book, you can even identify the trees they came from using the pictures in the book. The best time for collecting twigs is in February or March, long after trees have lost their leaves but before they have begun to bud. (Get permission to do the following!) Carefully cut twigs from a variety of trees (1 twig from each tree), and tape them to index cards. Write down the color and texture of the twig (these may change as the twig dries). Also, write down the name of the tree if you know it. Study the different characteristics of the twig parts using the magnifying glass, and compare them. Twig parts include the terminal bud (called the "bud" on our diagram) that will become new growth; bud scales to protect new leaves or flowers; leaf scars that show where stems of old leaves were attached; bud scale scars that show where last year's buds were and how much the twig grew over the year; bundle scars that show where sap flowed to leaves; lenticels, the tiny holes or openings through which bark "breathes"; and pith, the twig center. Make your own tree booklet: Use a hole punch to make 2 holes in the left side of each index card and tie the cards together with string or ribbon.

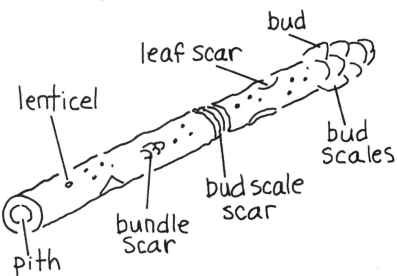

310

SECRET GARDEN

Grow a garden from secret seeds to see what pops up.

What You'll Need: 3 scoops of dirt from 3 different locations, spoon, shoe box lid, marker, plastic bags or plastic wrap, scissors, water, tape

Collect several spoonfuls of dirt from 3 different places. Keep the samples of soil separate. Divide the inside of a shoe box lid into 3 sections, and mark them off with a marker. Label each section with the name of the place where you collected the soil sample. Then line the lid with a plastic bag that has been cut open or a piece of plastic wrap. Place each sample of soil in the section with its place name. Sprinkle water over the soil in each section. Cover the lid with a piece of plastic wrap or another plastic bag. Seal the cover with tape to create a greenhouse. Set it in a sunny window and check every day or 2 for signs of any secret seeds.

SPORE PRINTS

311

Discover the tiny spores in a mushroom that can grow into new mushrooms.

What You'll Need: Mushrooms, white paper, black paper, knife, magnifying glass, bread, jar

Mature, ripe mushrooms can produce as many as 1,000,000 spores per minute for a period of several days! To see the mushroom spores, you will need 2 mature mushrooms or toadstools whose gills are exposed. (Have an adult help you choose mushrooms, or get adult permission for your mushroom or toadstool choices.) Cut the stems off the mushrooms. Place 1 mushroom on white paper and 1 on black paper. (The spores can be either black or white.) Leave the mushrooms on the paper overnight. After 24 hours, lift the mushrooms off the paper and check for spore prints. Use a magnifying glass to look more closely at the tiny mushroom-producing spores. Algae, lichen, moss, and mold are some other plants that grow from tiny spores. The tiny dustlike spores grow into plants when the conditions for growth are right. To explore spores further, put half a piece of bread in a jar. Sprinkle the bread with water, and cover the jar. Put the jar in a warm, dark place, and leave it there. You will be creating a warm, moist food source that will encourage growth of any tiny spores that might be in the air. After a few days take a look at the bread in the jar. What is happening? Do you see any growth? Caution: Wash your hands well after handling your experiment, and do NOT eat the results of either experiment!

FIND EARTH'S POLES

Make your own compass, and observe the magnetic pull of the poles.

What You'll Need: Modeling clay, pencil, horseshoe magnet, needle, waxed paper, scissors, bowl, water

Roll out a lump of modeling clay to form a firm base for a compass stand. Set the eraser end of the pencil in the base so the pencil is standing upright with the point up. Balance a horseshoe magnet on the tip of the pencil. Once balanced, the magnet will align itself on a north–south line. This happens because the earth itself acts as a huge magnet with lines of force running between the north and south poles. The compass automatically aligns itself with these invisible magnetic lines. You can also make a compass using a needle, a magnet, and a piece of waxed paper. Rub 1 end of the needle on the positive side of the magnet and 1 end on the negative side (run the needle in 1 direction only—not back and forth). Then cut a small circle of waxed paper, and stick the needle through the paper. Gently place the waxed paper in a bowl of water so it floats, and give it a spin. When the paper stops spinning, the needle will be lined up on a north–south line.

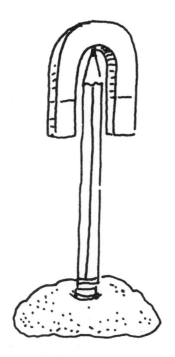

waxed paper

needle

TESTING BALANCE AND GRAVITY

Turn an experiment into a magic trick!

What You'll Need: Large index card, pencil, scissors, markers, paper clips, string

Cut out a symmetrical (both sides the same) upside-down clown, and watch how symmetry can work with gravity to create balance. To make a symmetrical clown, fold an index card in half and draw half of the clown. The fold line in the middle of the card is the middle of the clown. Cut out the clown, and unfold the paper. Decorate. Attach a paper clip to each arm for weight. Try balancing the clown on the eraser tip of a pencil. Then try balancing the clown with just 1 paper clip on 1 arm, and see if there is a different effect. Can you figure out the reason for the different results? To balance your clown on a tightrope, tie a string between 2 chairs or 2 legs of a table. Cut a notch in the clown's hat, and set the notch on the taut string.

FROZEN BUBBLES

Blow a soap bubble, then turn it into a delicate frozen orb.

What You'll Need: Measuring cup, soap powder, sugar, hot water, bowl, spoon or whisk, bubble wand

This is an activity for a cold, cold (below freezing) day when there is no wind in the air. Start by making a strong bubble solution. Mix ½ cup soap powder, ½ cup sugar, and 3 cups hot water. (This mixture will help the bubbles last longer.) Take the bubble solution and a bubble wand outside. Blow a bubble, and catch it on the wand. Let the bubble sit resting on the wand in the cold air. In the below-freezing chill, the bubble will soon freeze into a fragile crystal ball.

FULL TO THE RIM

315

Discover how many pins or pennies you can add to a full glass of water!

What You'll Need: Glass, pan with sides, water, pennies, sugar, teaspoon, straw

In this experiment, the surface tension of water will keep the water from overflowing, creating surprising results. Place the glass on a pan to catch spills. Fill the glass with water all the way to the rim. Make a guess about how many pennies you can add to the full glass. Then test by carefully inserting a penny slightly into the water and then letting go so it gently drops into the glass. Observe the top of the glass from the side so you can see the water level rising above the glass! Keep adding pennies until the water begins to overflow. The experiment can also be performed using sugar instead of pennies. Fill the glass to the top with water, and then add a teaspoon of sugar. Gently stir the water with a straw to dissolve the sugar. After the sugar is dissolved, add a second spoonful of sugar and stir, then a third, and a fourth! Perform the sugar experiment twice, first with cold water and then with hot, and compare the results.

WATER STRIDER

The water strider is an insect that uses the surface tension of water to its advantage. When it hunts for prey, its widely spaced feet help it run along the water's surface.

PINHOLE CAMERA

Unfortunately, this camera can't really take pictures. But you will learn something about how the human eye works.

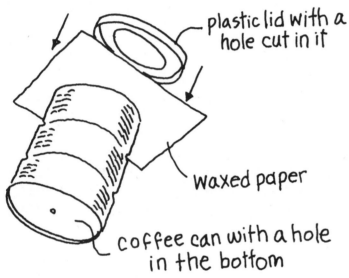

plastic lid with a hole cut in it

waxed paper

coffee can with a hole in the bottom

What You'll Need: Coffee can, nail, hammer, waxed paper, scissors, towel

Make a pinhole camera, and view an image inside the camera reversed in the same way an image appears reversed on the retina of the eye. To make the camera, have an adult help you hammer the nail through the middle of the coffee can's bottom. Remove the nail. Cut the center out of the plastic coffee-can lid. Cut a piece of waxed paper, approximately 8×8 inches, and place it over the open end of the can. Secure the waxed paper in place by putting the lid back on top of the can. Cover your head and the bottom (with the nail hole) of the camera with a towel, and look through the waxed paper end of the camera at an object. The object will appear upside down.

A YOUNG PHOTOGRAPHER

Ansel Adams, one of America's most famous photographers, knew at 14 that he wanted to be a photographer. He convinced his parents to take him to Yosemite National Park in the summer of 1916, and he began taking pictures. For the rest of his life, he returned to the park at least once a year to take pictures.

A GALLON A DAY

317

Perform an experiment to help you appreciate how much water you use every day.

What You'll Need: Plastic gallon container, water

To understand how vital water is to your daily existence, see if you can get by using only 1 gallon of water for 1 day. To prepare, fill a 1-gallon jug with water. Try to get through a whole day using only water from this gallon. That means you will be using water from the jug for hand washing, teeth brushing, face washing, dish rinsing, and drinking! Use the water sparingly, and see if you can make it last the whole day! Hint: Some of the water you can recycle, some you can't. Don't drink water you've used for washing your hands (or anything else, for that matter) or brushing your teeth. But you could use water you've washed your face in to wash your hands.

318

OCEAN IN A BOTTLE

Try a test on oil and water, then turn your experiment into a decorative display.

What You'll Need: Funnel, clear soda bottle, water, cooking oil, blue food coloring, glitter

Using a funnel, pour ½ cup of water and ½ cup of oil into a soda bottle. Put the lid on tightly, and shake the bottle vigorously to mix the substances. After shaking, put the bottle down and let it sit for a few minutes. What happens to the oil and water after you mix them? To turn your experiment into an ocean display, remove the top and add enough water to fill the bottle ⅔ full. Add a few drops of food coloring and some glitter, and shake the bottle gently to mix in the color. Then fill the rest of the bottle almost to the top with oil. Put the top back on tightly, and gently tilt the bottle back and forth to create an ocean wave effect.

WATERWHEEL IN MOTION

Make a miniature waterwheel, and put it to work under a water faucet.

What You'll Need: Empty plastic yogurt container, scissors, modeling clay, pencil, toothpick

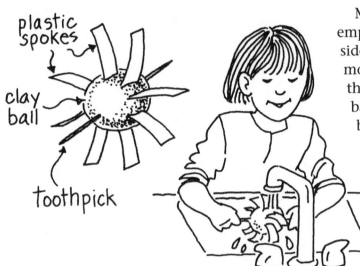

plastic spokes

clay ball

toothpick

Make spokes for your waterwheel from the sides of an empty yogurt container. Wash the container. Cut the sides of the container into 8 spokes. Then roll a lump of modeling clay into a ball about 2 inches across. Insert the spokes parallel to each another in a row around the ball of clay. Use the pencil to make a hole through the ball at a right angle to the row of spokes. Then insert the toothpick through the hole. Turn on a water faucet in a sink, and hold the waterwheel by the ends of the toothpick under the running water. The stream of water will turn the wheel.

CLEAN LIVING?

In Idaho Springs, Colorado, Charlie Tayler built a waterwheel in 1893 for gold mining. Mr. Tayler lived a long, healthy life, and he said it was because he never kissed women or took a bath!

MOUNT A LEAF COLLECTION

320

Gather a colorful collection of leaves, and mount them for display.

What You'll Need: Leaves, paper towel, newspaper, heavy books, glue, stiff paper, decoupage glue (available at an art or craft store), marker, hole punch, yarn

In fall, collect leaves in a wide array of colors or gather leaves of different shapes and sizes at any time during the year. After you have assembled the leaves, gently dry each with a paper towel to remove any moisture. Then set the leaves between layers of newspaper. Place heavy books on top, and weigh them down for 2 weeks. Then take the leaves out, and glue them to stiff paper. Paint the leaves with decoupage glue to strengthen them and give them a shiny surface. On each page, note the name of the tree the leaf came from as well as when and where the leaf was collected. Using the hole punch and yarn, tie the pages into a book.

EXPANDING HOT AIR

321

Perform a balloon experiment to see hot air expand.

What You'll Need: Bottle, pan, hot water, balloon, baking soda, vinegar

Stretch the end of a balloon over the top of a bottle. Set the bottle in a pan of hot water. After a few minutes the heat will cause the air in the balloon to expand, making the balloon begin to blow up. This happens because the hot water heats up the air inside the bottle. This causes the air to expand, filling up more space inside the balloon. You can also cause a balloon to inflate slightly by making carbon dioxide gas. Put a cupful of water into an empty soda bottle. Add a spoonful of baking soda. Pour in a little bit of vinegar, and quickly put a balloon over the bottle top. You can tell carbon dioxide has been created when you see the balloon expand slightly.

ANIMAL TRACKING

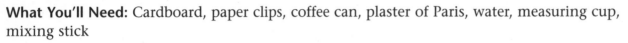

322

Find an animal track outside, and make a record of it.

What You'll Need: Cardboard, paper clips, coffee can, plaster of Paris, water, measuring cup, mixing stick

Search outdoors for a paw print or animal track left imprinted in the dirt. Using 4 strips of cardboard, make a square collar around the track by inserting the cardboard into the dirt surrounding it. Fold and clip the edges of the strips together to secure the collar, if needed. Mix the plaster of Paris with water in a coffee can according to the directions, and pour the plaster into the collar. Let the plaster set for ½ hour. Then lift the plaster out, and set it on newspaper with the track side facing up. Dry overnight. Now you have a permanent record of the animal track. (When you are done, throw out the coffee can; do not pour the remaining plaster of Paris into the sink!)

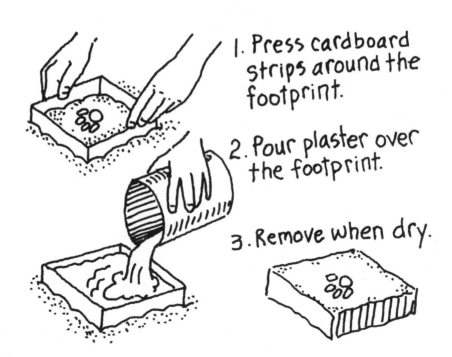

1. Press cardboard strips around the footprint.

2. Pour plaster over the footprint.

3. Remove when dry.

PAPER MAKING

323

Use plain old tissue to make your own paper!

What You'll Need: Tissues, bowl, water, measuring cup and spoon, eggbeater or blender, starch, shallow pan, piece of screen, newspaper, rolling pin

Tear up 4 pieces of tissue, and put them in a mixing bowl with 3 cups of hot water. Beat the paper and water with an eggbeater or put it in the blender. Mix until you have a smooth, watery texture. Then add a spoonful of starch to the mixture, and pour it into a shallow pan. Slide a piece of screen under the paper pulp, and lift it out of the pan. Hold it above the pan and let the extra water drip out. Then place the screen on a pile of newspaper. Put more newspaper on top. Use a rolling pin to roll over the newspaper pile to squeeze out the excess water. Roll back the top newspaper to expose the paper to the air. Let dry and take paper off screen. Then use the paper for writing, drawing, or a notecard. To make more decorative paper, add colored tissue paper to the mix before beating or mix in flower petals, glitter, or pieces of ribbon after the paper and water have been blended.

MAKING THE FIRST PAPER IN AMERICA

The first paper mill in North America was built by William Rittenhouse and William Bradford in 1690, on Wissahickon Creek, in Germantown, PA.

MINI TERRARIUM

324

clear
tape

seedling

moss
soil
gravel

Make your own little terrarium in a plastic cup, and watch tiny greenery grow.

What You'll Need: Plastic tablecloth or newspaper, 2 clear plastic cups, pebbles or gravel, potting soil, pitcher of water, seedlings, florist's moss, water-resistant tape

Cover the table with a plastic tablecloth or newspaper. Cover the bottom of a clear plastic cup with a layer of pebbles or gravel. Add a little more than an inch of potting soil above that. Sprinkle the soil with water to dampen it, and gently tamp it down. Make holes in the soil with your fingers for the seedlings, and place them in the holes. Carefully pack the soil around the seedlings. Cover the soil with moss, and water again to wet the soil. Place the second cup upside down on top of the first to create a greenhouse cover. Tape the second cup to the first. Set your mini greenhouse in a sunny spot, and watch your seedlings flourish.

Recycle, Recycle, Recycle

When you check to see if that plastic cup is recyclable, do you know what the number means? It refers to the type of plastic resin that is used to make the product. If you see the number 1, then this product can be recycled into bottles for cleaning products and nonfood items, egg cartons, and even for polyester fibers that are used in T-shirts, carpets, and fleece. Products with the number 2 on them can be recycled into flowerpots, toys, traffic cones, bottle carriers, and trash cans! Numbers 3 through 7 are not usually recyclable.

DROP AND SPLAT PAINTING

325

Put on a bathing suit or shorts and experiment outside on a warm summer day with drop painting.

What You'll Need: Plastic cups, water, food coloring, newspaper, paper, rocks, straws

Food coloring stains, so wear clothes your mom has approved! Fill several plastic cups with water. Take the cups and the rest of your materials outside. Add a few drops of food coloring to each cup to make different colors. Place a sheet of newspaper or a large piece of paper on the ground. You can put rocks on the corners to keep the paper in place. Put a straw in a cup of colored water, and place a thumb or finger over the top end of the straw. This will keep water inside the straw when you remove it from the cup. Lift the straw out of the cup and over the paper. Release your finger from the straw end so the colored water drops onto the paper. Experiment by raising straws full of water to different heights and observing how the height of the drop changes the resulting splat.

INDOOR RAIN

326

Perform an experiment to observe how rain is produced when warm, moist air rises up and hits the colder air above it.

What You'll Need: Jar with lid, hot water, ice cubes

Put a small amount of hot tap water in the jar. Place the lid upside down on top of the jar. Put several ice cubes inside the lid. You will be able to observe moisture forming on the lid top inside the jar, and soon you'll see the moisture drip down like rain. Warm air can hold more moisture than cold air. When warm air in the sky hits cold air higher up, it condenses, turns into water vapor, and rains!

GROWING UP

327

No matter how you try to fool them, seeds know which way is up!

What You'll Need: Glass or plastic jar, potting soil, lima bean seeds, water, black paper, tape, plastic wrap, rubber band

Fill a plastic or a glass jar with potting soil, and push a seed right next to the side of the jar where it can be easily seen. Place 3 more seeds around the jar where they can also be seen. Moisten the soil with water, and check daily to see if the seeds have begun to sprout. Once the seeds have sprouted, cover the outside of the jar with the black paper. Make a lid for the jar with plastic wrap and a rubber band. For the next 12 days you will be changing the position of the jar. During those 12 days, check the moisture level of the soil each day or 2 and add a little water whenever needed to keep the soil moist. To begin the position-changing experiment, lay the jar on its side for 3 days. After 3 days, turn the jar upside down and keep it that way for the next 3 days. Then lay the jar on its side again for 3 days. And finally, set the jar right side up for 3 days. After the 12 days of position changing, remove the black paper. You will discover that the beans kept changing their growth pattern in order to keep growing upward even though there was no light to show them which way was up.

WHAT'S IN IT?

A component of potting soil is usually peat moss. Peat moss is found in marshes, and it is sometimes burned for fuel. Through the years, peat moss has also been used for making diapers and for covering wounds!

IMAGINE THAT

Almost anything can be entertaining, whether you perform just for yourself, a few friends, or a whole audience. Think it would be fun to put on a show? In this chapter you'll find great ideas for everything you might need, including costumes, magic tricks, music, dance, talent show ideas, set decorations, play ideas, and publicity. If you're interested in simpler performances, you'll find lots of inspiration here, too. Once you've seen our suggestions, take a leap and spin off your own ideas. Don't worry about the final result—if you tried something different or new, then you succeeded. Imagine that!

MYSTERIOUS EYES MASK

328

Who says you're not a prince or princess? You'll look like one soon!

What You'll Need: Newspapers, simple mask that's worn around the eyes (or paper plate and scissors to make one), glue, feathers, glitter pen, brightly colored sheer fabric

Spread out the newspapers. If you don't have a mask that covers only the areas around the eyes, make one from a paper plate. Glue feathers to the mask or decorate it with jewel shapes made with a glitter pen. Add any other cool decorations you can think of—be as creative and unique as you like. Cut a piece of the sheer fabric to cover the lower part of your face. Glue the fabric to the back of the mask. Dazzle your audience with your mysterious eyes! Try other craft items to create different characters; use a bandana to look like an Old West bank robber.

DOUBLE DUTCH

Two ropes are twice as much fun as one!

What You'll Need: 2 extra-long jump ropes

This talent is exciting to watch—but it takes lots of patience to perfect your skills! You may already know someone who can do this. Or you might be able to find someone at school or in your neighborhood who knows a little. Learning and practicing is easier and more fun together than alone! Rhythm plays a big part in this talent, too. That's why there are so many rope-skipping rhymes. Chanting the rhymes helps you keep the beat and tells you when to jump. Get 2 friends to swing the ropes for you. Practice first with 1 rope, doing simple tricks such as hopping in a circle. Then add a second rope. Just do the same trick at a faster tempo. Check out other people's moves, and adapt them to make up your own stunts. Then practice stunts with 2 or 3 jumpers. Add fast music and you have a big crowd thriller!

JUGGLE THIS!

It takes patience to learn this skill, but your friends' amazement will make it all worthwhile!

What You'll Need: 3 small beanbags or soft balls

There are many different skills and talents; this one dates back to medieval times. Start with 1 beanbag or ball. Throw it from 1 hand to the other by making scooping loops in the air. Scoop it underhanded, then throw it in a "loop" over the opposite hand, about 2 inches over your head. Let it drop into the opposite palm. This "hang time" in the air is what gives you time to throw more balls or beanbags later. Make sure you throw the ball in loops directly over your body. If the loop veers forward, you may end up chasing balls! Now throw the ball in the same kind of loop from the opposite hand back to the first hand. Practice throwing it back and forth without stopping. Keep going until you feel an easy rhythm, almost like you could do this and talk at the same time. Now you're ready to add a second ball. Follow the same pattern as with 1 ball. When you're comfortable again, add a third ball. See, you're doing it!

331

THE FASHION SET

Doll up, dude up, and strut your stuff!

What You'll Need: Dress-up clothes (dresses, men's suits, shoes, hats, coats, purses, jewelry, gloves)

Borrow clothing from your parents, siblings, or any other people in your household. Be sure to ask for permission first! Now try dressing up as different people. See how many fashionable, funny, or downright strange outfits you can come up with. You'll have a roaring good time. Then plan a fashion show, and see if your audience can guess who you are!

CREATURE FEATURE

332

Make an appearance as your favorite animal!

What You'll Need: Paper bag or old mask, glue, scissors, 2 or 3 colors of felt, yarn in colors to match felt, black marker

Anything goes with this mask! Choose your favorite animal or create a weird new one. (If you're making a new mask with a paper bag, remember to cut holes for the eyes and mouth.) Glue pieces of felt to the mask for the base color of the face; let dry. Make more facial details out of different-colored felt, and glue them on. Let dry. Make eyebrows, short eyelashes, whiskers, and other details with the various colors of yarn. Add final details with the black marker.

WONDERFUL WIZARD OR CROWNED ROYALTY

You can be a wizard or the king or queen of your castle.

What You'll Need: Colored poster board; tape; clean, round, empty ice cream tub; pencil; yarn; gold star stickers; markers; poster paints; paintbrush; glitter glue; sheer or sparkly fabric; scissors; glue

Use the colored poster board to shape a cone for the wizard's hat; tape the cone in place. The ice cream tub is a perfect base for building a crown, or make a base out of posterboard. Don't worry if the base shapes of your hats are a little too small for your head; you can always make holes at the sides and tie the hats on with yarn. The decorations can be as plain or fancy as you wish. For the wizard's hat, use the gold star stickers, markers, poster paints, and glitter glue. When the decorations are dry, use glue or tape to fasten a corner of the sheer or sparkly fabric just inside the top of the hat. If you're making the king's or queen's crown, cut the poster board to make a saw-toothed strip. Glue the strip around the base of the ice cream tub to make the points, then bejewel and bedazzle your crown. Your audience awaits, your majesty!

COSTUME ORIGINS

People have been dressing up for thousands of years. Men and women would dance while wearing animal skins and masks that resembled animal faces. They danced to celebrate good hunting, plentiful crops, the birth of a child, and milestones in their lives. Some cultures still maintain that tradition today.

JUNIOR WIZARDS

334

Of course your stuffed animals can get into the act by dressing up, too.

What You'll Need: Colored poster board, pencil, scissors, glue, gold star stickers, markers, poster paints, paintbrush, glitter glue, masking tape, sheer or sparkly fabric, pencil, yarn

Your plush pets can look the part even if they can't learn any tricks. Follow the instructions for "Wonderful Wizard or Crowned Royalty." Try making smaller cones or use smaller round plastic containers. When each hat is finished, poke a hole on each side with a pencil. Tie the hats onto your stuffed animals with yarn. Best of all, these animals will keep their crowns on—you don't have to bribe them with treats.

335

PUPPET PARADISE

Make some fun puppets to perform with!

What You'll Need: Solid-color and patterned socks, old kitchen utensils, old pantyhose, cotton balls, wiggly eyes, poms, yarn, felt, white glue, glitter glue, multicolored glue, paint, paintbrushes

These puppets are so much fun to make, you may have enough ideas for a dozen of them. Take a good look at old pantyhose, gloves, and kitchen utensils, and try to picture what creatures you could turn them into—let your imagination run wild! A striped sock might become a sleek jungle tiger. A mitten could turn into a hairy spider. A hand beater might be a mad beautician with a whirling hairdo. Once you have a personality idea, use the craft materials to turn common household objects into fanciful puppets.

WHAT'S UP MY SLEEVE?

336

And now, ladies and gents, it's time for some magic!

What You'll Need: Round, empty oatmeal carton; paints; paintbrush; stickers; several old scarves; a large jacket

This trick works because the audience's attention is distracted by the magic carton. Remove the bottom of the carton. Decorate the carton with paint and let dry. Then add stickers with a magic theme. Tie the corners of the scarves together so that you have a long chain of them. Take 1 scarf and thread it under your shirt and through a sleeve, with the tip of a scarf corner just inside your sleeve cuff. Stuff the rest of the scarves inside the side of your shirt, underneath your arm. Pop on your magician's jacket, and produce your magic carton with a flourish. Let a member of the audience examine it to prove it's not rigged. "Prove" it further by sticking the hand with the loaded sleeve into it. While you're using your free hand to pull the carton from your arm, pull loose the scarf corner from your cuff. Do not take the carton completely off your arm, but let it sit in the palm of your hand, with your fingers steadying it. It will cover the edge of your cuff. Then reach into the carton with your free hand, grasp a corner of a scarf, and quickly pull out a rainbow of scarves! Your friends will be amazed and swear that the jacket is rigged. But you can let them examine that, too. You can also use string, rope, or yarn for variations on this trick. Hint: Be sure to practice this trick in front of a mirror until you can do it smoothly before you try it out on an audience.

HOW DID SHE DO THAT?

When 14-year-old Georgia magician Lulu Hearst started dazzling audiences with her tricks in 1895, experts from the world-famous Smithsonian Institution turned out to investigate. Even science could see the magic of magic!

I FEEL SOMETHING FURRY

Who knew so many animals could fit in this magic hat?

What You'll Need: One stuffed rabbit and other plush animals, small cardboard box, solid-color fabric remnant and felt the same color, pencil, glue, scissors, black poster board, black electrical tape

This trick uses the same principle as "What's Up My Sleeve?" The rabbit isn't actually in the hat. You're going to pull it from somewhere else. Cut a hole in the bottom of the cardboard box. It should be big enough for your hand and anything you want to pull out of the hat, but probably no wider than 5 inches across. Then cut off the flaps around the top. This will serve as a platform for your hat, and it will hide the rabbit—and everything else you pull out of the hat. Put the box on a table (hole side up), and drape the fabric over it. With a pencil, trace the hole on the fabric. Cut out the hole. Cut a square of felt just large enough to cover the hole. Cover the hole with the felt, and glue 1 edge of the felt square to the fabric.

Make a top hat out of the black poster board. Cut a strip about 6 or 7 inches tall and long enough to fit around your head. Tape that piece together to form a cylinder, and place it standing up on the poster board. Trace around the circle and cut it out; this will be the top of the hat. To make the hat brim, draw a circle around the one you've just cut out, and then draw another one about 3 inches larger. Cut out the outer circle and then cut out the inner circle, which will leave you with a large donut shape. Tape this brim to the hat with the black electrical tape. Tape the top of the hat on only halfway around. When you perform, use a tiny strip of tape on the open end to make the hat appear closed.

For your magic trick, hide all your beanbag animals or other objects under the box. Then drape the fabric over it, centering the felt-covered hole over the hole in the box. Bow and tip your hat to your audience, showing them that there is absolutely nothing in it. Set your magic hat on top of the box, and wave your magic wand. Reach into the hat, breaking open the small piece of tape, and reach through the felt into the box. Stick your arm in up to your elbow and "root around" in the hat for that silly rabbit. Start pulling out everything else but the rabbit. Say, "No, I didn't want a tiger (or whatever animal you pull out). Where is that rabbit?" The suspense builds until . . . out pops the rabbit!

PLAYING WITH SPOONS

338

Hurray for spoons! What an easy "instrument" to play.

What You'll Need: Old spoon, ridged metal can, metal kitchen grater

Run a spoon up and down the ridges of a metal can. You'll get a nice sound. Try sliding it across all the textures of a metal kitchen grater. (Be careful not to slide your fingers on the grater!) Think of other kitchen objects that you could use with a spoon to make music. Create your own song using all these instruments, and write your own lyrics. Then perform your musical melody for your family and friends.

339

BUTCHER, BAKER, CANDLESTICK MAKER

Have fun acting out different careers. Try them all!

What You'll Need: Old clothes donated for costumes or clothes bought at yard sales or thrift stores (then washed before wearing), newspaper, construction paper, scissors, markers, stapler, clear tape, glue, cardboard

Make your own costumes for various jobs, such as a doctor, nurse, firefighter, lawyer, schoolteacher, and so on. You could use secondhand clothes or cut the costume pieces out of newspaper or construction paper. If you're making your own clothes, decorate the paper pieces with markers. Fasten them with staples, clear tape, and glue. Use the cardboard to cut out props, such as stethoscopes, swords, shields, computers, and so on. Don't forget to create really fun hats to go along with your costumes! Do this just for fun or put on a show for your friends.

GOTTA TAP!

340

Ever see Gene Kelly's dance routine in the old movie Singing in the Rain*? Or Gregory Hines in the movie* White Nights*? That, my friends, is tap!*

What You'll Need: Comfortable, old pair of shoes; self-adhesive metal heel clips from the shoe accessories department; concrete floor, patio, or sidewalk; your favorite music

Make your feet sing, just like in the old-time Broadway and Hollywood musicals. Ask permission to turn an old pair of shoes into tap shoes by attaching self-adhesive metal heel clips. (Don't use nails!) Attach the clips to the toes, balls of the foot, and heels. Tap dancers use these and other areas of the foot while doing their step combinations.

For beginning tap, first practice walking only on the balls of your feet, with your heels in the air. Like the sound? To place only the ball of 1 foot on the floor is called a "step." Transfer your weight to the ball of 1 foot and let your heel down with a "click" sound. This is called a "heel." Try this beginning combination slowly: While standing in place, step right, heel right. Step left, heel left. Step right, heel right. Step left, heel left. Practice it until you feel a rhythm. When you feel comfortable, try picking up speed. Try walking that way with music. Very cool, huh? You might even want to try a beginning class just for fun.

FAVORITE MUSICAL
Gene Kelly's famous musical *Singing in the Rain* was named the tenth most popular movie ever made by the American Film Institute's 100 Years, 100 Movies Celebration.

ROCKIN' AND ROLLIN' WAVES

Rolling ocean waves always make a big splash—not to mention adding a really cool touch to your production.

What You'll Need: Heavy-duty scissors, 3 big cardboard boxes of the same size, duct tape, newspapers, old shirts, poster paints, paintbrushes, 6 paper towel tubes

These look fantastic when they're done. You may want an adult's help with this group project at first, but then you'll be able to make your own waves. Use the heavy-duty scissors to cut out the bottom of a box and cut down 1 corner of the box from top to bottom. Spread the box out, and cut off all the flaps. Do the same with the other boxes. Using 1 of the discarded flaps and a pencil, sketch a big curl of an ocean wave. Cut it out. This is your wave template. Use the template to trace waves across each of the long cardboard strips you've made out of the boxes. Make sure there's at least 10 to 12 inches of space under each wave. Now cut out your rows of waves.

Next, wrap the duct tape from top to bottom around the bent parts in each row of waves. This stabilizes the rows. To make a sturdy handle, cut down the length of a paper towel tube. Roll the cardboard into a tighter tube (until there's a double layer of cardboard all the way around), and wrap the tube in duct tape. Do the same with the other tubes. To attach the handles to a row of waves, lay 1 tube at the end of 1 row, on the back side. Half of it should be behind the wave and half below it. Tape the handle to the cardboard. The tape can be overlapped to the front, since you are going to paint it anyway. Do the same at the other end of the row.

Spread out the newspapers, and put on your old shirt. Paint a base color on your waves and let dry. Then add details in several different colors. When your waves are finished, line up the lengths of waves, 1 in front of the other. One person will hold each handle. The middle row should be held a little higher than the front one, and the back row a little higher than the middle one. Practice making the front and back rows sway in 1 direction while the middle row sways in the opposite direction. Talk about awesome wave action!

MIGHTY MASKS

342

These easy-to-make masks look hilarious!

What You'll Need: Several old magazines to cut up, scissors, thin paper plates, glue, pencil, yarn

Leaf through old magazines, and cut out individual facial features from pictures of faces. Divide them into piles of ears, noses, eyebrows, chins, hair, heads, etc. Don't forget animal faces! Cut eye and mouth holes out of a paper plate. Pick out a goofy arrangement of facial features, and glue them onto the plate to make a mask. Let the glue dry. Next, punch holes in the sides of the mask with a pencil. Tie a piece of yarn to the hole on each side to hold the mask on your head. Admire the crazy results.

343

MYSTERY

Everyone loves a mystery, especially trying to guess whodunit before the play is over!

Rewrite a short classic mystery story as a play with modern characters and situations. Hunt for costumes in thrift stores and at garage sales. This will keep you busy for at least a month! Practice by yourselves, then try out the play on a small audience to get helpful feedback. Refine your performance and take it to a larger audience.

GRANDMA, WHAT BIG TEETH YOU HAVE!

344

Who says theater has to be serious?

What You'll Need: Costumes

Fairy tales are some of the best things to perform because the audience recognizes the story. Pick a favorite fairy tale to make into a play. Have fun with the script and spoof or exaggerate the story. Retell the ending the way you think it should have ended. Some of the funniest plays are written this way. Gather some hilarious costumes, and practice the play with a straight face, if you can! When you've achieved perfection, get ready to make your audience roar with laughter.

345 # PLAY IT YOUR WAY

Who says you can't bring big Broadway musicals to your school auditorium or living room?

What You'll Need: Costumes

Choose a musical that most people in your audience would like. Then rewrite the story, and set the scene at your school. Narrow the play down, and use just 2 or 3 musical numbers. You could also rewrite the song lyrics. Add costumes, singing (or lip-synching if you're not using new words), and dancing, and you may just bring the house down!

SOUND THAT STRETCHES

346

Strumming was never so fun!

What You'll Need: Large, empty margarine tub or metal coffee can; stickers; lots of rubber bands; empty tissue box

Have an adult help you with this project. Decorate either the margarine tub or the metal coffee can with your favorite stickers. Then stretch 5 to 7 rubber bands around the container so that they go over the open end. Practice plucking! Notice how a rubber band makes a high-pitched sound when pulled tightly across the top? It sounds deeper when you loosen it. How does the sound change when you use an empty tissue box instead? Try tuning your "sounds that stretch."

347

SHAKE IT UP, BABY

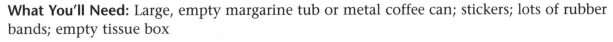

Try making your own instruments!

What You'll Need: 3 teaspoons uncooked rice, dried beans, 2 empty diet shake cans or soda cans, clear packing tape, pencil, paper, scissors, markers or stickers

Put the rice in an empty diet shake can (soda cans don't last as long, but they will work for this project). Remove the tab and seal the opening with clear packing tape. If you like, make your own cool label for the can. To make the label, cut a piece of paper 9 inches long and 4½ inches wide. Decorate the label with markers or stickers. Tape 1 side of the label to the can. Then make small rolls of tape and stick them between the label and the can. Wrap the label around the can so that the loose end overlaps the taped end, and tape down the loose end. Put dried beans in the other can, and make a decorated label for that one, too. Try using the rice can for a lighter sound and the bean can for a louder sound. Start shaking!

HIDDEN COIN

348

You should be making a million dollars, because you can find money anywhere!

What You'll Need: 2 quarters

   This trick takes a little practice. Ask someone to stand up in front with you. While the audience's attention is on the person coming forward, slip a quarter far enough into 1 sleeve so that it doesn't slide out. Be careful never to let this hand drop to your side. Move fast! Then both you and the participant should face the group, but you should be slightly facing one another. Make sure no one can see your back. Now, hold out both palms for everyone to see. Put the second quarter on 1 palm. Then put your hands behind your back and count "1, 2, 3" while pretending to switch the quarter from hand to hand behind your back. Actually, you slip the quarter down your waistband. (Hint: Your shirt must be tucked in to do this.) Bring your closed fists forward for the participant to choose. They tap 1 fist: "Darn, it's empty." You open the other fist—surprise, it's empty, too! Say, "Now where is that quarter? Hmm." Keep talking while you finally drop the hand where the quarter is hidden. Wiggle the hand behind your back until you feel the quarter slide into your palm. With the quarter in your loosely closed fist, reach up behind your participant's ear and exclaim, "Hey, how did that get there?" Then show the quarter.

RECORD THE RECORDER

Or tape the trumpet! Play and record any instrument or style of music just for the fun of it.

What You'll Need: Musical instrument, tape recorder and tape

Try an instrument that you're familiar with or experiment with a new one. Anything goes. Try out different styles, such as jazz, blues, rap, pop, rock, or simple folk songs. Follow the instructions that came with the instrument, and practice a few times before recording. Then put a tape in the recorder, and hit the record button. Listening to yourself play makes mastering an instrument easier. You could also practice a special song, and then use it as background music for your next musical show! Write your own music or use your favorite song.

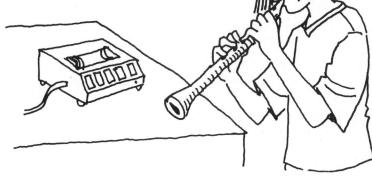

PUPPET PAGEANT

Use puppets to perform a funny skit or silly song.

What You'll Need: Handmade puppets

Choose a skit or song you already know or make one up. If none of the puppets you made go with your skit or song, create some new ones to match! Practice holding your arm straight up in the air for long periods of time. Try to work up to 10 minutes—you'll need the stamina when you put on your show. To make sock puppet characters look realistic when they talk, move only your thumb, not your fingers. After all, wouldn't we look funny if we moved the top of our heads when we talked?

FLYERS, POSTERS, INVITATIONS, TICKETS, AND PROGRAMS

351

Now that you've gone to all the trouble to put on a show, let the world know about it!

What You'll Need: Typewriter or computer, white and colored paper, copy machine, poster board, markers, gift wrap, envelopes, stamps, heavy card stock, scissors

Flyers and Posters: Type up your announcement on the typewriter or computer. Add computer graphic art, if you can. Next, print it on white paper, then take it to a copy store and print the fliers in bright colors. Post them wherever your audience will be. Finally, paint or draw some special posters to go in high-traffic areas where lots of people will see them. Ask for permission before posting the flyers and posters.

Invitations: Follow the basic instructions for the flyers and posters. If you don't have access to computer graphic art, cut out colorful pictures from gift wrap that fit the theme of your show, and glue them on the invitations. Decorate the outside of the envelopes, too, if you like. Then address, stamp, and mail the invitations.

Tickets: Use little information on the ticket, and make it easy to read. Include the name of the show, location, time, day of the week, date, and "presented by" information. Print or make one original of the ticket. Check it carefully! Now make more copies of the ticket on the same page. Then copy or print your page on colored paper. Cut the tickets apart and hand them out.

Programs: Make enough programs for everyone in the audience. If you have a computer, explore type styles to find a fun one for the show title. Place the show title at the top of the page. Below it, list the acts in the show and names of the actors in each. Then list everyone who helped with the presentation. Make sure you thank any sponsors who helped you put on your show and mention what they donated. Let the show begin!

RING THOSE BELLS

352

All you have to do is move to make musical sounds.

What You'll Need: 26 mini jingle bells, hair scrunchies, needle and thread, large margarine tub lid, hole punch, brightly colored yarn scraps

To make 2 bell anklets, sew 8 bells around each hair scrunchie. Put them on your ankles, and dance up a storm. To make a tambourine, cut out the middle of the lid. Then use the hole punch to punch out 10 evenly spaced holes around the edge of the lid. Tie on the bells with the yarn scraps. Play in time to music on the radio or make up your own jingly tune!

PANTOMIME

353

Try acting out a story without words!

What You'll Need: White mime makeup (optional), makeup, clothing in all 1 color, background music (optional)

Write a very simple story, or choose a piece of instrumental music. Then use your imagination to show the story you hear in it. If you can get some, put on the classic white mime makeup. If not, ask permission to use some makeup to highlight your eyes and mouth. Also, make sure to pull your hair away from your face. This helps the audience see your expressions better. Choose a color and wear it from head to toe so the emphasis will be on the story you are miming, not the costume. Now act out your story using exaggerated facial expressions and body movements.

SILENT MOVIE

354

Your miming skills will come in handy here!

What You'll Need: Poster boards, thick black marker, background music, video camera

Choose a simple story you and your friends know or make one up. Now make it into a movie script. Make each scene fairly short, and write each actor's lines for the scene on a poster board with the black marker. Have everyone rehearse and act out their parts while saying their lines aloud. Turn off the sound on the video camera, and film the first scene. Next, shoot a close-up of the poster board with the actors' lines written on it. Do the same for the rest of the scenes. The film will look like an old silent movie where the actors' lips moved but no voices were heard. Playing background music while you watch will make the experience even more like a silent movie. And if you can speed up the film just a little, it will make everyone laugh out loud. When the film is done, play it backward!

355

SODA BOTTLE "PIPE ORGAN"

This is so cool your friends may want to try it.

What You'll Need: Newspapers, 5 or 6 empty glass soda bottles, water, dark-colored nail polish, food coloring

Spread out the newspapers. Practice making a tone by blowing into the top of a glass soda bottle. When you have it mastered, fill the bottles with different levels of water. (If you've had some music lessons, you could try tuning the bottles to specific notes.) Arrange the bottles from left to right, low notes to high notes. Practice playing an easy song. Make a water level mark on each bottle with dark-colored nail polish. (Mark the notes, too, if you know them.) Let the polish dry. Using a drop or 2 of food coloring, put a different color in each bottle. Put your thumb over the end of each bottle, and gently swirl the water to mix the color in. Now you can practice your songs on your soda bottle pipe organ!

PUPPET STAGE

356

Even puppets need a stage to show off their talents!

What You'll Need: 2 brooms, masking tape, 3 chairs, 3 old belts, blankets or bedspreads

Here's how to make a stage for your puppet show. Ask an adult's permission to borrow 2 brooms. Lay them on the floor end to end, with the handles overlapping each other by 4 inches. Wrap the handles together with lots of masking tape. Next, arrange 2 chairs about 2 yards apart with their backs facing each other. Set the broom pole on the chairs, with the straw part of the brooms resting on the chair backs. Prop a third chair, facing the audience, under the part where the broom handles are taped together. Use a belt to wrap the broom pole to the top part of the chair back. Do this at both ends of the broom pole with the other belts. This makes your stage more stable. Throw blankets or bedspreads over the broom pole for curtains. Sit behind the stage, raise your puppets above the broom poles, and let the show begin!

357

"TWIRLIES"

These bright umbrellas are fun to paint and add lots of eye appeal to your play or dance routine.

What You'll Need: Old umbrellas, newspapers, old shirt, poster paints, paintbrushes

Get your parents' permission to paint the umbrellas. Spread out lots of newspapers, and slip into your old shirt. Open up the umbrellas. You may give an umbrella a new base color if you wish, or use the original color if it's a bright one. Wait a few hours for the paint to dry. Then paint a wild pattern in a contrasting color. Try spirals, dots, zigzags, and other shapes. If you want, you can also paint the inside of the umbrella a solid color. Use the umbrellas in a show. You can have people crouch behind the decorated umbrellas and spin them for interesting backgrounds. Or have dancers dance around them, twirl them, and use them as props. (For eye safety, make sure each umbrella twirler is standing a good distance away from the next person!)

BALLET BRAINSTORM

358

Looking graceful and flowing with the music can be hard work, but the results are worth it.

What You'll Need: Soft, flexible shoes or socks; music from your favorite ballet; smooth floor; mirror (optional)

It's very important to begin slowly by stretching out your arms, torso, back, legs, ankles, and feet. Don't bounce. Listen to the music as you warm up your muscles. Imagine what you might do with each part of the music. When you're done warming up, start the music again and use your body to "interpret" what you hear. How would you move to soft parts? How would you move to fast, dramatic parts?

359

LE JAZZ HOT

Move to your own groove!

What You'll Need: Comfortable shoes, fast or slow jazz music, smooth floor, mirror (optional)

Explore some types of jazz music—have an adult help you find radio stations that play jazz. Find the kind of music you feel like dancing to. Listen to the rhythm, and then try to follow it with your feet and other parts of your body. Be creative! If you want, practice in front of a mirror to refine your moves. You "interpret" the music with your steps and with your movements.

STORY SCROLL

360

Make one of these and you'll really be on a roll!

What You'll Need: White butcher paper, 2 long gift wrap tubes, cardboard box, scissors, markers or paints

Choose a folktale or a play you've seen, or make up your own story. Find a TV-size box, and cut out a screen-size hole in the front. Cut round holes in the top and bottom of the left-hand and right-hand corners, so you can thread the gift wrap tubes through the holes. Next, pick 10 key scenes in the story. Draw or paint the scenes from the story in panels on the white butcher paper. Make sure the panels fit the size of the TV "screen." Don't forget to make a title page and a closing page. The pictures can be done by several people, if you wish, and then taped together later in the correct order. Thread the gift wrap tubes through the holes above and below the "screen." Once the artwork is finished and taped together, tape the ends of the scroll onto the tubes. Roll the scroll around the tubes. Choose a narrator to tell the story while someone rolls the panels forward.

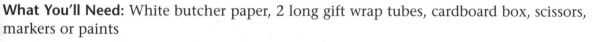

ANCIENT SCROLLS

Probably the most famous scrolls in the world are the Dead Sea Scrolls. They were found by a young Bedouin shepherd in the Judean Desert when he was searching for a lost goat. He entered a cave and found ancient clay jars filled with some of the scrolls.

STAR SEARCH

361

The next big star could be you!

If you want to put on a talent show, you'll need all different kinds of acts. Learn a song or 2, or come up with a really funny comedy routine. You'll want to place these solo acts between the group numbers. If you're a singer, try performing your number in the character of the person the song is about and in costume. If you're a comedian, practice your timing and try to use topics that everyone can relate to; you'll "hook" your audience early on. Have your friends audition for the show with their special solo acts. Hint: You may have heard it before, but professionals do it, too—practice in front of a mirror. It will give you more confidence later.

THE "SHELL" GAME

362

Here's a twist—let the audience try to fool you.

What You'll Need: 3 cups, any object

You can do this with a table in front of an audience or around a dinner table. The "trick" is to pick a secret partner who won't spill the secret. Tell your friends you have developed amazing powers of X-ray vision. Arrange 3 cups in a row, and ask a person to hide an object under a cup while your back is turned. Then have him or her mix up the cups several times. Whirl around and face the cups with a flourish. Glance at your partner out of the corner of your eye. If his or her hand is on his or her left hip, the object is hidden under the cup on the left. If the hand is on the right hip, the object is under the cup on the right. Both hands on the hips means the object is under the middle cup. Whip the cup up and away from the object, and declare, "Aha!" Then ask your amazed audience if someone would care to try to stump you. Repeat the trick several times. Your friends will be totally perplexed!

WHEREFORE ART THOU ROMEO?

Ah, the romance of a dramatic balcony scene!

What You'll Need: Heavy-duty scissors, cardboard refrigerator box, duct tape, newspapers, old shirt, poster paints, paintbrushes, bricks or concrete blocks, scrap fabric (optional), aerobic step bench or small step stool

Many dramatic plays have a balcony scene. Here's how you can carry off yours. You may want an adult to help you with some parts. Using the heavy-duty scissors, cut out all the way down 1 corner of the box. You will have 3 vertical "bends" in your box where the corners used to be. Lay the box on the floor, and bend up the left and right bends, leaving the middle 1 flat. At the left and right bends, tape the upper flaps together to form corners. (Don't do anything with the lower flaps yet.) Stand the box up, and reinforce the corners, from top to bottom, with tape. Then tape together the middle flaps at the top, but do not bend them.

About 6 inches from the very top of the box, draw your balcony window. Make it 2×2 feet. Have an adult help you poke the scissors into a corner of the window, and cut it out. Spread the newspapers out under the box. Bend the bottom flaps to the inside. These are the "feet" for your balcony. The corner flaps will overlap the middle flaps. Tape these together, then put bricks or concrete blocks on the flaps to stabilize the balcony. Now for the messy part. Put on your old shirt, get out the paint, and go! Paint a base color and let dry. If you want bushes or flowers at the foot of the balcony, paint those in next. Finally, with a color darker than the base color, brush in the outlines of bricks or stones. Then add curtains if you wish. Inside the balcony, put an aerobic step or small step stool beneath the window. Step up to the window, and make your speech to thundering applause!

"SYNCH" YOU VERY MUCH

364

For those with a touch of stage fright (that would be most of us!), lip-synching a song is much easier than actually singing it live.

What You'll Need: Tape of a favorite song, tape player, instrument props, creative costumes, video camera (optional)

In addition to the pretend singing, dressing up like the band or person that really sings the song is a blast. Not to mention the amusing instrument props you can make. Or the added hamming it up you can do! For a variation, try filming a video of your lip-synch act. You'll have less stage fear and more time to be creative. Act out the story behind the song without pretending to sing it. If your audience roars with applause and laughter, you'll know you have succeeded.

365

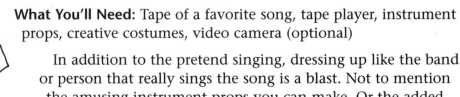

STAGE CYCLING

For a "wheely" good act, practice, practice, practice!

What You'll Need: Bicycles and/or unicycles, safety pads and helmets, basketball and hoop, juggling objects

With practice, cycling is another talent show crowd-pleaser. Gather a group of friends, and work up a routine for you and your bikes. For example, ride in formation and cross paths with each other (just like motorcycle police officers in parades). For those with access to and ability to ride a unicycle, try playing 1-on-1 basketball or juggling at the same time. Make sure you wear bicycle helmets and pads at all times and observe safety rules! Also for safety's sake, have an adult supervise your practices and performances. We've said it before: Practice, practice, practice makes perfect!

INDEX